Forgiving the Devil:

Coming to Terms with Damaged Relationships

Forgiving the Devil:

Coming to Terms with Damaged Relationships

by

Terry D. Hargrave, Ph.D.

Zeig, Tucker & Theisen, Inc.
Phoenix, Arizona

Library of Congress Cataloging-in-Publication Data

Hargrave, Terry D.
    Forgiving the devil : coming to terms with damaged relationships / by
Terry D. Hargrave.
        p. cm.
    ISBN 1-891944-45-2 (alk. paper)
    1. Forgiveness. 2. Family. 3. Interpersonal communication. 4. Inter-
generational relations. 5. Intergenerational communication. 6. Family
psychotherapy. I. Title.
BF637.F67 H375 2001
158.2--dc21   2001045514

Published by

ZEIG, TUCKER & THEISEN, INC.
3614 North 24th Street
Phoenix, AZ 85016

Manufactured in the United States of America

10 9 8 7 6 5 4 3 2

Contents

SECTION THREE
Questions Concerning the Work of Forgiveness

Acknowledgments

The landscape for forgiveness has changed dramatically in the eight years since I first started talking about my work in this area. Initially, my words were met with some resistance and fear, but as they listened more closely, both professionals and lay people expressed relief and confidence that forgiveness in healing family and other important relationships had the right "feel." For the lay reader who wishes to join the trek to improve relationships through forgiveness and for the professional who will help guide the journey, this book is written to highlight the markers along the way.

I want to acknowledge those people who have encouraged my effort: First, my wife, who has loved and supported me through my endeavor to understand this exciting new and old framework. Next, my family of origin, especially my parents, who taught me firsthand how to try to forgive. Finally, my clients and workshop participants, who have put my ideas into practice.

Section One

Beginning the Work of Forgiveness

1

The Work of Forgiveness

"If we are going to do the job right, this is where we need to cut you." These are the words that echo from underneath a scarred over, painful wound that lies deep in my psyche. These words represent the "watershed" in my life where I came to the terrible conclusion that my family did not love me and that they were not trustworthy.

For many of us, the relationships that shaped us were dangerous places. When we lean into the memories of these relationships, we may find heinous acts such as incest, physical abuse, emotional manipulation. The people from these relationships are threatening manipulators who robbed us of our emotional stability and infect us with doubt and insecurity. If we have these types of relationships in our pasts, then likely there are similar relationships in which we are currently involved. These relationships are with people whom we may love, but we may find that even simple interactions are difficult as we struggle to act in trustworthy and loving ways.

When I hear the stories of people who have experienced such pain, my first inclination is to shy away, hide, and hope that I can soon forget the story so my nausea will go away. But these people cannot forget. They live every day with the way these experiences have molded, and to some extent ruined, their lives. How do they go on? How do they get past such heinous acts committed against them?

This book is about forgiveness. Forgiveness is necessary because relationships always define who we are and how we act. If we really want to feel better about ourselves and act differently in our relationships, it will be necessary to go back and redress those relationships that damaged our lives and taught and defined incorrect and erroneous information about who we are and how we should act.

THREE PERSONAL MEMORIES

In order to talk about the work of forgiveness, I must always return to the personal place where the pain, and then reconciliation, of relationships began. My story revolves around a series of memories that wash through my mind like waves. The first memory is of a time when I was eight. I was the fourth of four children, and my mother and father were struggling hard to keep life together on an even keel. My mother had married my father on a whim when she was 16 and he was 21, because she did not want to go home and tell her father that she had been expelled from school. My father gladly eloped with my mother because he was deeply in love and also was anxious to escape the life of the dreary New Mexico town where they lived. We four children were born over the next seven years. After a failed attempt at farming, my parents came to the courageous decision to pursue teaching degrees to improve their prospects. My mother earned her high school equivalency diploma and started college, while my father worked two and three jobs to see her to a successful graduation and a secure job. He then finished his college degree and began his teaching career.

Something, however, was desperately wrong in my family. The stress of my parents' working endless hours, trying to make financial ends meet, and raising four children ranging in age from 8 to 15 was taking its toll. Childhood survivors of the Depression, financial bankruptcy early in their marriage, my parents had come back together after a yearlong separation in the interest of keeping our family intact. But in spite of all this effort and commitment, there was still a feeling of desperate hopelessness in the family. My parents were emotionally immature, and at times manipulative and physically abusive to each other and to us as children. Certainly, they did many things right; we were always fed and clothed, and they made extraordinary attempts to improve our lives. But the times that they were out of control — the beatings, burning, raging, leaving — left me with the impression that I was not loved and not wanted. The family was unsafe, and I saw no prospect of recapturing its security and promise.

At the age of eight and somewhat depressed, I decided to end it all. I went into my family's bathroom and selected one of my father's double-edged razor blades. Carefully, I sliced into my forearm. I knew that if I cut into my wrist, I would really be in trouble and might die! Looking back, I realize, of course, that I wanted a declaration that my family loved me and never wanted me to try such a thing again. But when my mother discovered what I had done, the result was quite different. She jerked my skinny arm up to her eye level, took the razor to my wrist and made the terrible statement that dominated my belief about love and trust for a third of my life: "If we want to do the job right, we need to cut you here." She did not cut, but she left the room in a rage and me with a toxic shame permeating my being. I had wanted a declaration of love, but what I had received was a blunt statement that convinced me that not only was I not loved, I was not wanted — and my family would be better off without me. For the rest of my years at home I laid very low, never venturing out to discover whether my family felt differently. My sister and my two brothers bolted or drifted from my family of origin much in the same way that I did, carrying the damage of the past and desperately trying to make life better.

The second memory emerges around 1984 at the death of my maternal grandfather. I had gone on with my life and part of me was really okay. I had married and was beginning to get some sense of career direction where I could make a contribution. I had some good friends and some good times, but there was still a part of me that I had to keep blocked off and hidden away. No one really knew me, including my wife, because there were just too many terrible thoughts there. I felt a burden of incompetence and became threatened and defensive at the least suggestion. I protected myself emotionally from friends by keeping to myself and reducing to a trickle the amount of emotional nurture and commitment I gave them. I decided not to have children partly because I did not want to pass along the abuse that I had experienced as a child, but mainly out of my desire not to have to share my wife's nurturing of me with anyone else. Most disturbing to me, however, was my relationship with my wife. I would feel desperately dependent on her love and affection, and at the same time would want her to stay out of my space and leave me alone. In her presence, I would feel shamefully needy of her and yet angry at her encroaching on my life, both emotionally and physically. These things I kept to myself, laboring with the reality that all was not as good on the inside as it looked on the outside.

I traveled with my wife and my mother to see my grandfather for what I knew would be the very last time. I had very little to do with him over that weekend and remember very little of the time. I do, however, have a very vivid memory of my last words to him. As we were getting ready to leave, I stepped up to my grandfather's bedside and said something like, "Take care of yourself." My mother then patted her father's hand and said, "Daddy, I will see you next week." But then my wife, Sharon, who had experienced the extreme pain of losing loved ones to suicide, sickness, and murder without having had the opportunity to say goodbye, took his enormous round head into both of her hands, looked tenderly into his eyes, and said, "I love you, and I will miss you."

I glanced at my grandfather as he stiffened, not knowing what to say. Then I looked at my mother, who was feeling the same tenseness. I became painfully aware of my own anxiety. Sharon had revealed the heart of the pain in my family in her moment of tenderness. I had had many issues with my grandfather. He had always expressed extreme disappointment at my inability to perform up to his expectations. He seldom called me by my name;

instead, he often called me by my brother's name. He failed to come to my wedding or recognize any other accomplishment in my life. I had never experienced an intimate moment with him, and had never seen him have an intimate moment with anyone else. In short, all these issues represented what I felt was his lack of care and nurture for me and, in response, my lack of love for him. As we stood beside my grandfather's deathbed on that day, I realized that this was the same issue that lay between my grandfather and my mother. Painfully and realistically, I also came to realize that it was that same lack of caring that stood between my mother and myself. No words were spoken. We left my grandfather's house for the last time. For me, the pain was beyond normal grief.

Not long after we left, I was able to acknowledge that the words my wife had spoken had been what I wished I could have said. The opportunity to work things out was gone, however, and I would never see him again. But I knew that I faced the same issue with my mother, and that one day she and my father inevitably would lie on their own deathbeds. I wanted to be in the position by then where I would no longer be imprisoned by secrecy and confusion and would be able to say to them, all issues resolved: "I love you, and I will miss you." But to do so would mean that I would have to open myself up to the wounds that had been inflicted in the past. I began to work in earnest to make sense of my abused childhood and to grow through the pain I faced as an adult.

I did not confront my parents immediately, nor did I make dramatic moves to "work things out." I did a significant amount of reading, went to some therapy, and had small discussions with my family to ascertain if there was any potential for establishing a more loving and trusting relationship. After five years or so, we had made significant progress. I had become more open and did not feel nearly as threatened. I had learned to achieve a more balanced life with Sharon in the sense of my being okay as an individual while also being intimately connected to her. My parents and I had moved along to the point where we were able to be together without feeling tense about impending conflict. Although we had not discussed every issue related to my growing up in an abusive place, we had talked about enough instances for which they acknowledged some responsibility that I knew they wanted to make things better. And things were better. My parents had become older, wiser, and more nurturing, and I had reached a place where I could work through some of my anger and get some of the answers I needed.

The third memory surfaced a few years ago, when I was visiting my parents while on a trip. My mother had retired from teaching and was now tutoring students. I observed her with one student and saw how caring, patient, and helpful she was. When I questioned her about why she exhibited those qualities now when she hadn't with me and my siblings when we were younger, she laughingly replied, "I had so many things to worry about with you kids, like the length of your hair and whether or not you would be good people. With this kid, all I have to worry about is if he can pass biology!" But she then became very serious and said, "You know, I never knew how important it was to rock and cuddle children. I didn't have that when I was young, so I never did it for any of you. There is a lack of nurturing that comes from my side of the family." I listened to her words and parked them in my mind.

A few months later, my parents came to visit my home upon the birth of my second child. I had come to love the process of putting my first child to sleep, as much for myself as for her. I would rock her in a quiet, subdued room and gently sing to her, "Hush, little baby, don't say a word. Papa's gonna' buy you a mockin' bird . . . ." One evening during my parents' visit, while I was rocking my newborn son, I noticed the silhouette of my mother in the hall, listening and rocking back and forth as I sang.

Later that year, my mother and father went on a mission trip to Brazil with their Presbyterian church group. After the mission was over, part of the group returned to the United States and others, including my parents, stayed behind to do some touring. At the time, I was moving my family back to the area where my parents lived, and one of our friends who had been on the mission trip dropped by to see us. She commented, "Your mother is such a loving and nurturing woman." My mother and I certainly were different now, but I still found it extremely difficult to perceive that much change. The look on my face must have communicated exactly what I was feeling. "My mother? Loving? Nurturing? You must have her mixed up with someone else." But then the friend told the story. My mother had chosen as her mission the children who had tuberculosis and were quarantined in the hospital. For six or seven hours a day, my mother would rock, cuddle, and sing to children who would be separated from their families for months. I asked my mother about the story upon her return, and she said, "If I had it to do all over again, that is what I would have done for you."

My mother and father were loving and trustworthy people. I suspect that they always had been, and that they were finally able to overcome their own issues of damage enough to access those resources and give them to me. And as I watch my mother and father rock, hold, and cuddle my children, and hold me as they do, I experience the empowerment of nurture. It strengthens me to be a better person, husband, and father. It strengthens my whole intergenerational group.

FORGIVENESS DEFINED

One of my fundamental beliefs is that people are hurt by relationships and healed by relationships. Family relationships, because they are the first relationships in which we engage and everything we learn in the world is in that context of family, are the most powerful in terms of potential damage and healing. We must be clear, however, about what forgiveness means. *Forgiveness is the process by which love and trust are reestablished in relationships.* Forgiveness doesn't consist of simple platitudes or superficial statements that are expected to make the past go away. It is not forgetting about serious damage or letting someone off who caused hurt without taking responsibility. It is not about subjecting yourself to an untrustworthy or unloving person who will just hurt you all over again. What forgiveness is about is the coming together of at least two people, after there has been severe damage or hurt in their relationship, to rewrite the story of love and trust in a responsible way that will make their relationships and families stronger and healthier.

Two things make families work: love and trust. The way my family loves me tells me about who I am. They are the first people — and perhaps the only ones — who have the opportunity to love me unconditionally. When you are born into a family, you can do nothing for yourself, and certainly can do nothing to benefit your family. You require constant attention. In response to their many sacrifices, you may be colicky and cry constantly. You may disturb everyone in your new family group. But if that family continues to care for you, to cuddle and nurture you despite the trouble you cause, then you learn that you are someone special. You have no claim to their good will and love, but they give it to you because they are thankful for your being in their lives. You are loved. Through your family's love, you learn that you are worthy as an individual and important not for what you can do, but for who you are.

Love is an important part of family relationships, but it is not the whole story. The second necessary component of family is trust. As I grow, I see how individuals in the group make personal sacrifices and give of themselves for the good of the family. In return, the family provides encouragement and safety to the individual members. I learn by watching and experience that it is my responsibility to look out for the family and that it is fair for me to expect that they will help me grow and accomplish my individual goals. I learn to give to my family what they need because I trust that they will give me what I need. In this balance of giving and receiving, I learn how to act responsibly in relationships. I learn how to trust.

Thus, basically, there are two questions we ask of our family and of most primary relationships: *Do you love me? Are you trustworthy?* Most people would answer the questions with a qualified

"Yes," because no family is perfect and may have done things to us and treated us in ways that could not be characterized by total unconditional acceptance and love. Nonetheless, the family — perhaps more than any other relationship — aspires to this unconditional love. Parents constantly make sacrifices for their children. Spouses commit to each other and then go about the endless task of invoking humility and compromise to attain the peace of intimacy with the human being they chose as a companion. Children maintain an intense loyalty to their families, believing that their existence depends on the family processes they learned. Even though our families may not be perfect, most experience the relationships as places of safety, security, and love. Relational or emotional hurts inflicted by members of these families are like the cuts, bruises, and scrapes that we suffered as children. They hurt — sometimes intensely — and then they heal, leaving no pain and little or no scarring.

But for those of us who answer the question, "Does my family love me and is my family trustworthy?" with an unqualified "No," the word "family" is a painful reminder of a lack of security, sacrifice, and stability. As children, we were expected to act as adults and take care of our parents emotionally. And those parents felt justified in being more concerned about their own emotional and physical happiness than with ours. Sacrifice does not come easily to spent parents who resent the fact that they receive little or no recognition or compensation for their efforts. The spouses tend to expect each other to make up for the personal deficits that exist in themselves. When these efforts fail, they become more manipulative and threatening. In these families, looking out for oneself is the only way to survive. The hurts are severe, like those engendered by the amputation of limbs or the removal of organs.

Family damage can come in many forms: physical or emotional abuse, neglect, or addictions. But the reality that makes this pain so severe is the underlying influence that our families do not love us and are not trustworthy. Without a change in the family relationship, we are doomed to live our lives in the hopeless pain

of not being loved and not being able to trust or be trusted in relationships. It is in families like these that the work of forgiveness
is needed and can be powerful. It has the potential of making a
secure place where we can know that we are loved and that we
can trust.

Why should we forgive? We want to know that we are loved
and that people are trustworthy. Shame, rage, guilt, and fear over-
whelm us if we believe otherwise. But the task of forgiving takes
enormous courage, because we may re-enter relationships only to
find that our families still do not love us and still cannot be
trusted. If we cut ourselves off from our families, however, we
lock in all those toxic feelings about ourselves and relationships.
The question becomes this: How do we help ourselves by the
work of forgiveness and use its power to restore love and trust to
change our feelings and beliefs?

THE WORK OF FORGIVENESS

The work of forgiveness in families can be said to fit two broad
categories: *salvage* and *restoration*. Salvage and restoration are related concepts, and neither is inherently better than the other. Salvage is the use of forgiveness to gain insight into how to keep the
damage done in the past from continuing to affect one's life, now
and in the future. It means understanding the circumstances of the
abused, and abuser, so that one does not carry the burden of pain
alone. Think of salvage as a ship that has struck an iceberg and
sunk. If the hole in the ship is too large and the water is too deep,
the ship will never be restored to a seaworthy condition. But
there are things that can be salvaged from the ship to use in other
ships. Also, lessons learned from the accident will serve to avoid
future mishaps. In other words, some relationships are too damaged to be repaired and made useful again. Often, the person who
caused us hurt is not trustworthy and may hurt us again. Or, the
person who was relationally irresponsible may have died or be
otherwise unavailable, in which case it is not possible to restore
love and trust by re-engaging in the relationship. However, there

is forgiveness work that can be done through salvage. The victim can learn to recognize the interactions that were damaging and prevent them from happening again. The person damaged in the relationship can also use that damage as a lesson in how to make future relationships more loving and trustworthy. Finally, the victim can gain an understanding of his or her victimizer that correctly assigns responsibility for the damage caused and relieves much of the ensuing emotional pain. Salvage in the work of forgiveness does not restore love and trust to the damaged relationship, but it does help ensure their presence in future relationships. Salvage efforts involve two stations of forgiveness: *insight* and *understanding*.

Restoration differs from salvage in that it requires the person who has been wronged in a relationship to put himself or herself in a position where love and trust can be rebuilt by the person who perpetuated the hurt. Again, using our ship illustration, a ship hits an iceberg and sinks. This time, if the hole is not too large or the water too deep, the damage can be repaired and the ship refloated. Although it was damaged, the ship can be returned to the service for which it was intended.

Restoration means that after a severe violation has taken place and the relationship has "sunk," the victim and victimizer work together to restore love and trust and make the relationship functional again. This, of course, involves risk, as the damaging acts may reoccur. Trust in the relationship is at risk. For restoration to result, the victimized person must be given legitimate reason to believe that the wrongdoer accepts responsibility for the injustice and hurt he or she caused, while promising to refrain from further such actions. It is accomplished when the victim no longer has to hold the wrongdoer responsible for the injustice; the wrongdoer holds himself or herself responsible. The relationship between the two can then be reestablished because trust has been restored. Restoration involves allowing the wrongdoer to compensate for past injustices by being trustworthy in the future, and also by overtly addressing the responsibility for the injustice. Thus, restoration is accomplished by *giving the opportunity for compensation* and by *overt forgiving*.

The work of forgiveness, therefore, can be divided into the two broad categories of *salvage* and *restoration*, as shown in Figure 1.1. Salvage has two stations, *insight* and *understanding*, whereas restoration's two stations are *giving the opportunity for compensation* and *overt forgiving*. Even though the work of forgiveness is the goal of both salvage and restoration, the two are very different and are appropriate in different relationships at different times. Also, even though there are four stations in the work of forgiveness, they are not *stages* in that one precedes or follows another. The work of forgiveness in the four stations is, of course, intertwined, but one must not assume that it moves from one station to the next. People usually oscillate among these stations many times in the course of the same relationship. The stations of forgiveness are simply constructs to help us to better understand the work of forgiveness.

THE WORK OF FORGIVENESS			
Salvage		Restoration	
Insight	Under-standing	Giving the Opportunity for Compensation	Overt Forgiving

Figure 1.1.
The Four Stations of Forgiveness

DID IT REALLY HAPPEN?

I return to the memories of reconciliation and forgiveness in my family many times. I sometimes wonder, "Is all this restoration for real? Did it really happen?" A few months ago, my oldest sibling, my sister, lay dying of cancer. As in many families, not all of my siblings were able to work through past issues of abuse as I had. My sister had eloped just after graduating from high school and had six children. Although my parents and my sister had made some efforts to stay connected through the years, their relationship had never lost the tense feeling of judgement. My sister did not want to open herself up to improving the relationship because she feared that it would result in additional hurt. My parents would become weary from making efforts that would, in the end, be criticized as being "too little, too late." So, in the last few years, my sister had drifted far outside the family group. But when the call came that she was going to die, my parents once again mobilized their efforts. For the final eight months of my sister's life, they were there doing all they could to take care of her physically. My sister, not having anything to fear any longer, received and responded to their care with heartfelt attachment. I have memories of my father and mother cuddling with her on her bed. I can still see my mother reading stories to my sister. I can hear their quiet moans and prayers together.

The last time I saw my sister was on her 47th birthday. As it happened, my whole family of origin — my parents and two brothers as well as myself — were in her room alone for about thirty minutes. We laughed together, talking about our favorite memories of one another. We spoke about the things we would miss and the things that we liked best about each other. Finally, it was time to leave. My sister took my hand and said, "We really are a family, aren't we?" I kissed her on the lips, stared into her eyes and said, "I love you, I will miss you, and I will never forget you."

Family is where we return to deal with relationships. It may enable us to do better and make loving and nurturing connections, or it may remind us of insidious damage and make it difficult for us to relate at all. In my family group, the ability to lean into my parents and eventually find that they were loving and trustworthy people enabled me to give to my family in unselfish and caring ways. It enabled my sister to finish her life stronger. It enabled my group to become a family.

The work of forgiveness is not easy or perfect. It is difficult work that leaves many questions about pain and victimization unanswered. But I know from my own family history that forgiveness can redress old relationships, even the most painful ones, to the point where they can be nurturing. I know that when it comes my parents' time to die, I will feel empowered by their legacy of love and trust, just a I did on the day I said goodbye to my sister and told her, "I love you, and I will never forget you. I will miss you."

Special Focus One:
How Have You Been Hurt?

You might take a few moments before you read on to focus on some of the following statements.

1. How have you been hurt in your family? Was it a violation of love, a violation of trust, or both?

2. Who is the person (or persons) most responsible for the violations in your life?

3. What are the "watershed" events in your life that represent the violations you experienced? (Stories or events that capture the characteristics of what you experienced.)

2

The Roots of Family Pain

"My mother was a crazy, sick woman. She didn't want to have anything to do with her husband and she gave me to him. Look at me! I'm 42 and I'm an old woman! Everything that I was, everything that I could ever be, has been taken away! I had to take care of my sister when I was young so I never got a childhood. I had to marry a man I didn't love because my stepfather got me pregnant. I've been physically, sexually, and emotionally abused every year of my life! I can't get anything I want because what I want is for things to go back and be right. I can't get back my past and there is nothing left. My mother took everything I was and threw it away. How can I go on? How can I forgive such evil?"

Maybe the hurt you feel is greater than this woman's pain, and maybe it is less. But the hurt that we feel from damaging and broken family relationships can leave us hopeless, angry, despairing, and even vengeful. Indeed, how can we forgive such evil when the very people that we trusted to love and nurture us treated us instead with acts of abuse and damaging manipulation? Families are the place where we depend on safe haven. They are the relationships we depend on the most to love and nurture us.

When our relationships damage us, whether it is by abuse, neglect, threats or manipulation, it confuses us and leaves us on our own with no secure place. Where do I go and what do I do to find that safe place where people love me and give to me freely if my family has damaged me? How do we move on? How do we heal from such damage?

In order to get to the point of forgiveness and moving on, it is first necessary to understand our pain. Pain comes from the violation of love and trust, and forgiveness is about reestablishing that love and trust in a relationship. To forgive the violation, you must know what the violation is all about.

As I have said before, family relationships are unique in their ability to tell us about ourselves. It is only in relationships that we discover that we are lovable and that dealings with people are safe. When any relationship, especially the family, damages us, the pain is more severe because we learn that the very people who are supposed to accept us for who we are do not do so. We are not lovable and, therefore, we become confused about who we are. But their irresponsibility also models for us that we cannot act normally in relationships. Family relationships and future relationships may cause similar pain and hurt. Instead of freely giving to others, I must take action that will protect myself. Thus, in its most elemental form, the root of family pain is a violation of love and trust. In my family, I came to the conclusion that I was not a lovable person and that my family did not want me. I shamed myself for being unlovable and put up a firm wall between myself and others so that they could not hurt me again. I labored in the pain of loneliness.

FAMILY VIOLATIONS AND PAIN

Violations of Love

One of the memories that I hope will be etched into my brain is the peace I felt at the birth of my first child. I remember holding my little girl only a few hours after she was born and my wife resting at my side in a quiet room. Here she was, the physical representation of the intimacy that my wife and I shared. Genetically half me and half my wife, she was testimony to our struggle to contribute to a relationship that would bind us together. Such intimacy requires not only commitment, but also humility, as we lose a little bit of ourselves in the relationship to gain what the other has to offer. The fact that my daughter represented our intimacy was special, but the fact that out of that intimacy was born a whole new life was astounding. She was perfect. Unique. Special. Precious. All the things that were the best parts of human family relationships were rooted in this new little one, unscathed by the world. She was easy to love.

When we come into the world, we have no ability to perceive ourselves. As we grow, our cognitive structures start allowing us to formulate an idea of who we are, and we become self-aware. But we do not perceive ourselves by ourselves; we borrow from our caretaker's perception of us. We are driven to discover an answer to the question, "Who am I?" If our families treat us in ways that are loving, nurturing, accepting, and intense, then we will begin to answer that we are lovable, worthwhile, acceptable, and extraordinary. When we are loved, we achieve a sense of self that is well-measured and balanced. If, however, we were in families that were unloving, withholding, rigid, and neglectful, our answer to the question of "Who am I?" will indeed be different. We will feel unlovable, shameful, unworthy, and never able to measure up to the most meager of expectations.

We are totally dependent on the care and love of our family to make this program positive. I believe, as do many others, that human beings are extraordinary and precious. I feel that we are not worthwhile because of what we as individuals do, but because we represent the only species that is able to analyze its actions and think in abstractions. We have the capacity to look at situations, even distasteful ones, and be hopeful for the future. There is a dignity about the human spirit that cannot be denied no matter how people are treated. I am reminded of these truths when I think about the courageous struggle of the Holocaust victims in World War II. People are unique and special in their beings, not because of their actions.

Family violations of love are heinous because they rob us of our sense of self. We have only this one opportunity for the original programing of ourselves to take place. Because we are special and unique, we deserve to be treated with love and dignity. My children are genetic representations of my life and that of my wife. Loving them is like loving the representations of ourselves. To regard them with contempt or to neglect them is to forget our own personhood and how they are our fruit. My children deserve my love not only because they are human, but because they are part of me. When I withhold that love, I violate who they are. In essence, I say, "There is nothing very special about you; you are not any more unique than I am, and you will learn to think of yourself in this limited way." To receive such a violation of love from your family is like a curse. You may encounter many people in your life — friends, teachers, spouses — who will tell you that you are special, but you will always carry this original software from those who should have found it easiest to love you and should have loved you the most. It is a curse to never know why your family did not find it easy or irresistible to love you.

Violations of Trust

Family violations and pain come in so many forms that it is often difficult for us to decipher where the relational damage occurred. I have found a theoretical construct called contextual family therapy (Boszormenyi-Nagy & Krasner, 1986) to be particularly helpful in conceptualizing how relational damage originates and how it affects the individual and the family. The main idea of this construct centers on the view that we, as humans, are dependent on relationships in order to experience self-understanding and self-awareness. We are built in such a way that as we interact in relationships, we have an innate sense of justice that demands that we try to balance what we are entitled to receive from a relationship and what we are obligated to give in order to maintain it. In very simple terms, in every relationship we are entitled to take something for ourselves and are obligated to give something back to the other person. The give and take in a relationship should be balanced in such a way as to uphold our sense of justice or fairness. As family members interact, we are interdependent. This requires us to assume responsibility for our actions, accept the consequences of how we carry out a relationship, and strive for fairness and balance in the relationship's give and take.

If we can say that relationships rely on a balance of this obligation (give) and merit (take), we can illustrate them by setting them up like a bookkeeping account in a ledger. Figure 2.1 illustrates such an account for a relationship between myself and my wife. The left side of the ledger account would represent the merit (take) that I am entitled to receive from my wife: respect, care, and spousal intimacy. I am entitled to these things partly because that is what husbands and wives provide in our society, but mostly because I am expected, or obligated, to give those same things to my wife that she is expected, or obligated, to give to me. On the right side of the ledger, my obligations (give) that maintain the relationship are listed. Here you find the same obligation to my wife that I am entitled to receive. The relationship is balanced, symmetrical, and fair, as my wife and I give to each other.

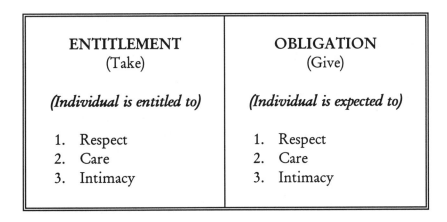

ENTITLEMENT (Take)	OBLIGATION (Give)
(Individual is entitled to)	*(Individual is expected to)*
1. Respect	1. Respect
2. Care	2. Care
3. Intimacy	3. Intimacy

Figure 2.1.
Example of a Husband and Wife Relational Ledger

When have we have this type of balance between giving what the relationship requires and receiving that to which we are entitled, then the sense of fairness is satisfied. As this balance between give and take continues over time, we experience trustworthiness in each other. As we experience trust, we are enabled to give to the other. In other words, as I do my part in my relationship with Sharon and she does hers, I give freely because I trust that she will give me what I need. I do not have to threaten her or manipulate her to get it. When my trust level is high, I work on fulfilling my obligations, confident that my just entitlement will be fulfilled.

When relationships are put into this context of fairness regarding give and take, we can understand the function of human emotions. Emotions are simple barometers or gauges that give us a reading on the status of balance between relational give and take. When we do not receive what we deserve, we become angry. On the other hand, when we are overly compensated by a relationship to which we have not contributed, we may feel guilty. The balance of give and take in any relationship includes the emotional field of both the individual and family relationships.

Trustworthiness either is accrued or depleted in relationships. You can see how this works in the example of the husband and wife. For example, say Sharon wanted to go to a secluded mountain cabin for a few months to write a novel. She would be entirely removed from the family and certainly would not be contributing her fair share to the relationship. The burden of care and responsibility for the family would fall on me. However, since we have had many years of balanced and fair relating, I would agree that my wife should go because I believe that she would do the same for me if I were to make such a request. I would have a large reserve of trust that would enable the relationship to continue as it was, even though it would be unbalanced for several months. I fulfill the extra obligation because I trust that my wife would do the same for me if our roles were reversed. However, if the reserve of trust between the two of us had not been built, it would be unlikely that I would willingly agree to her going.

Trust, however, is never a static resource. Just because I trust my wife today and have enough trust in reserve to accept her not contributing to the relationship for awhile does not mean that it will never be a problem. For instance, if after three months of working on her book she asked for another three months, I might agree, but not be so amenable to the idea. If, at the end of that time, she refused to come home, I might find my trust resource depleted because of the extended period of living in an imbalance of give and take. I would feel denied my entitlement from the relationship and probably be unwilling to give freely. I might make some threats or be manipulative in order to get my wife to come home. Trust is built by balanced and fair relationships and is depleted when relationships are imbalanced. Even the best of relationships are endangered when trust is gone.

It is fairly easy to see how trustworthiness and balance are built and maintained in *horizontal* relationships — in those between equals such as spouses, friends, or siblings. Give and take in such relationships are symmetrical and balanced. But there is a second type of relationship where balance and fairness are asymmetrical. These are called *vertical* relationships and exist between generations, such as parents, children, and grandparents. Figure 2.2 is an example of a relationship ledger account between a parent and an infant. The left side of the ledger shows just a few of the things that the parent is obligated to give to a child. However, there is really no entitlement or merit that the parent receives from the infant, except for great emotional satisfaction. The fact remains that the parent would not be justified in withholding what he or she is obligated to give to the child no matter how the child acts.

While most of us would agree that the account is imbalanced, we would also agree that it is a fair relationship. It is fair because the parent was once an infant and the benefactor of the same love, care, nurture, security, protection, and discipline that he or she now gives. By fulfilling the obligation to provide such care for the infant, the parent earns merit by obligating the child to pass along such care to his or her own children. In these vertical relationships, the fairness is maintained down through succeeding generations. When we fulfill obligations to children, we empower the children to do the same thing for their children and ensure that the family will become stronger.

Trustworthiness in vertical relationships is continued through successive generations.

ENTITLEMENT (Take)	OBLIGATION (Give)
(Individual is entitled to)	*(Individual is expected to)*
1. Love 2. Care 3. Nurture 4. Security 5. Protection 6. Discipline	No Required Obligation

Figure 2.2.
Example of a Parent and Child Relational Ledger

What happens if a child does not get what he or she is entitled to because the parent does not fulfill the obligations? This is often the case, and to complicate matters, the child may then be required to fulfill obligations that are not the child's. For instance, a six-year-old child might be expected to love and nurture a parent rather than the other way around. In these cases, the damage becomes severe, because as the child falters in his or her ability to provide adult-like love and care, the parent becomes more manipulative, threatening, and abusive. As the child grows, he or she does not forget the just entitlement he or she was owed. The hurt stays buried inside until the child, as an adult, becomes powerful enough to demand that someone else fulfill the missed entitlement from childhood. Of course, the prime candidates to get this obligation put onto them is the person's spouse or children. The person would then withhold nurture and love, threatening or manipulating his or her own children to love and nurture. This in turn robs a new generation of the fair entitlement, and the beat of abuse and damaging families goes on. Trustworthiness is drained off and evaporated from these families, leaving a painful violation intact. Where there is a lack of trust, people refuse to give to each other because they believe that it will deplete their resources, and they become destructive in demanding or manipulating people into giving to them.

Special Focus Two:
Understanding Your Pain

1. Try to set up a ledger account that reflects the relationship that caused you pain.

ENTITLEMENT (Take) *(Individual is entitled to)*	OBLIGATION (Give) *(Individual is expected to)*

2. Is the ledger accurate?

3. How would you like the account to change?

4.   What would have to happen to make the relationship trust-
     worthy once more?

5.   If it could change, are you willing for such a change to
     happen?

Results of Violations of Love and Trust

    You are entitled to receive love and trust from your family,
and it causes deep pain when it isn't provided. If you are like
most people I see, you transform that pain into feelings about
yourself (primarily violations of love) and beliefs about actions
you must take in future relationships (primarily violations of
trust). As Figure 2.3 illustrates, when you are violated, you are
likely to feel (1) resulting rage as you experience uncontrolled anger toward your victimizer, or (2) shame as you accuse yourself of
being unlovable and not deserving of a trustworthy relationship.
Similarly, you are likely to take actions in future relationships
that are (1) overcontrolling as you try to minimize your risk of
hurt, or (2) chaotic as you assume that little can be done to form
trusting relationships and that you will eventually be hurt despite
any effort.

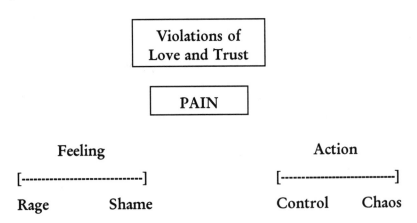

Figure 2.3.
Model of Violations of Love and Trust

Pain that results from relationships where one is not given the love and trust he or she deserves is hard-biting and severe. It insults everything we instinctively feel that families should give us. When we are subjected to this kind of pain, we cannot help but ask: Why was I not loved? Why was my family not trustworthy? What do I do now? How we answer these questions largely determines how we deal with and cover up the pain we feel.

Rage. Some of us will answer the first two questions by blaming our victimizer with unreasonable vigor. Our initial reaction may be that we just cannot understand how a father could abuse his daughter sexually or how a mother could be so unfeeling as to burn her son as punishment. But as we are reexposed and revictimized by a family member, we begin thinking that the perpetrator's actions are so unjustifiable as to be beyond human reason. From this point, it is one step to the belief that the person who is victimizing us is not human at all because of the atrocities he or she has meted out to us. We begin to view this person as a devil or a monster. We see our victimizers not for their humanity with its goodness and flaws, but as depraved and evil. Such a feeling pushes us past anger and indignation at our victimizers' actions and into a rage that demands that as they have forfeited their rights as human beings, they must be treated as evil scum. Consider how this woman sees her alcoholic mother who was absent and neglectful of her and her brother and sister when they were children.

> "She isn't a human being according to my definition. She is perfect evil. She only consumes for her own pleasure and does not have one concern for another living thing. Like a shark or Hitler, she destroys for her own desires. There is nothing redeemable in her."

When we feel this type of rage concerning the actions of the people who hurt us, we become unreasonable in our approach to reality. We know that we have been hurt and that someone is responsible for this overwhelming pain we feel. But since the reason for the destructive action makes no sense, we tend to disconnect our reason and let our pain dictate that our victimizers must have been unfeeling and irrational monsters. Therefore, we feel our rage is justified. Monsters have no reason. They are, after all, built to do harm. There is only one way to handle them, and that is to kill or isolate them without regard to their thoughts or feelings.

History is replete with displays of this type of rage toward humans who damage others. In history, we need look no further back than our century to find political tyrants like Idi Amin, Joseph Stalin, or Adolf Hitler to hate. More recently, we have been horrified by the unconscionable acts of the likes of Timothy McVeigh and Jeffrey Dahmer, who killed and injured others for their own gratification or to further their own selfish cause.

Undoubtedly, there are some evil people who have sacrificed their humanity to their destructive appetites. I believe, however, that these are very few. Most victimizers and perpetrators who violate us, seemingly without thought or regard, are fallible human beings just like you and me. We are all capable of acts of evil, as well as of acts of great good. That is what humanity and individual choice are all about. Most people who hurt have not lost their humanity, but have made damaging choices for which they must be held responsible. If we, as victims, succumb to this defensive rage, we are thrown into a similar unthinking frenzy that will allow us to commit evil acts of aggression not only against our victimizers, but also against other innocent people. Anger and indignation in reaction to the way that someone has mistreated or abused us may be justified in our effort to hold them responsible, but rage puts us out of touch with our own humanity and places those who commit evil acts beyond the bounds of responsibility.

Shame. Others will answer the question of "Why was I not loved?" or "Why was my family not trustworthy?" by pointing the finger at themselves. We conclude that the fault for the unreasonable or manipulative action lies not with our families, but with the fact that we were not worthy to be treated any other way.

To believe that we deserved to be neglected or abused by our families is to be filled with a toxic shame that penetrates our soul and colors every interaction. A healthy self-image is impossible to attain when this type of shame is present. We believe that those who should have loved us unconditionally found it impossible to do so because we were faulty. Our being, our image, was unacceptable. No matter what we do or how hard we try in the future to compensate for our lack, we still fall short of being acceptable. It is not that we believe that we were tainted or poisoned by our actions; we believe that we ourselves are the poison and taint every relationship or situation we encounter. When something goes wrong in a relationship, it is our fault. It must be our fault because we know how lacking or "bad" we really are.

Handling family violations by internalizing this shame results in relationships that are stilted and unrealistic. People who feel such shame go to great lengths to please families that are irresponsible and unreasonable. Like the 45-year-old woman who as a girl was repeatedly sexually abused by her father, people who feel shame will try anything to become more acceptable.

> "Every time I go to my parents' house, it is like I have to know that I am okay. I will bring them presents, cook them meals, clean their house, anything to make them happy. If he [the father] looks at me with that displeased look, I just feel like I have to make up for his disappointment in me. I've apologized a thousand times and not known why I was apologizing. I guess I was apologizing for being myself, someone that he thought wasn't good enough for him."

Shame can be so great that it will cause us to accept responsibility for even the most heinous of acts. Physically abused women will take the blame for their husbands' beating them and refuse to press charges. Sexually abused people will condemn themselves for their terrible actions while worrying that they were not satisfying to the person who molested them. Shame can so skew a person's thinking that the person will not be able to believe that he or she is worthy of living in a happy, safe, secure, or emotionally nurturing place, and so will find it impossible to leave abusive situations.

Shame is so insidious because it cuts us off from who we really are and sets us adrift in relativity. If I am not deserving of love and have no right to rely on trust, then I am set outside the normal justice of human relationships. I feel as if I am a "no count"; that is, I do not count as a human being. If I am cut loose as a human being, then I become dependent and hopeless in that I will take whatever people will give to me because I am desperate. However, because I feel I deserve nothing, I suffer guilt for whatever I take. I feel hopeless because I find little in life that does not make me feel either guilty or anxious.

Rage and Shame Cycles. Of course, it is possible that many of us will be what I call *turn stylers*. We flip-flop in cycles of intense rage and shame. We may be swept away by our unreasoning rage over being abused and damaged and feel justified in lashing out at the "monsters" who damaged us or the current bystanders who remind us of the people who caused us pain. After the dust settles and we view the results of our self-justifying binge, perhaps the crushed egos of the people we have assaulted with words or the mangled bodies and properties that were physically attacked, then we feel the backlash of remorse and self-condemnation of one who could carry out such despicable acts. We drift into distance, depression, and despondency. Then, after we again have been ignored or taken advantage of, we rise up again in righteous indignation. Consider the story of a physically abusive man who was emotionally neglected as a child.

> "I truly do hate myself after I explode all over my wife. I think of how worthless and undeserving I am of any love or affection from her. I feel ashamed of who I am and what I've done. But almost in the same instance, I will feel so angry that I feel that way about myself. I feel like I deserve some respect and happiness and that it is unfair that I have had to put up with all the stuff that I have had to. I will

feel like I am spinning around inside myself feeling ashamed and feeling like smashing something. It seems like I'm flying apart."

There is no balance in these types of cycles. Both rage and shame are extreme reactions in our attempts to deal with the pain of not being loved or having a trustworthy family. When we oscillate between these extremes, we find it impossible to find any security or happiness, and others are unable to have a relationship with us because of our dual nature. Even caring people who really do wish to help are thrown off by our erratic behavior. When we feel shame, they see us as pitiful, sad dogs that seem to want comfort but who, when these people reach out their hands to pet them, turn into raging, rabid animals that return their loving gestures by biting them.

Control. When the relationships on which you depend most prove unreliable or cause you hurt, how are you to act in other relationships? Anyone, no matter how seemingly harmless or well meaning, has the potential of hurting me terribly. Hurt causes pain, and if I hate pain enough, I will find ways to avoid it at almost any cost.

When violations of trust take place in my closest relationships, it upsets my balance of what I can reasonably expect from people when I relate to them. Instead of expecting the freedom to give — you give me what I need and I give you what you need — I foresee the necessity to protect myself so that you will not take advantage of me. At the root of my pain is the fear that I will be exploited. Therefore, I will have no trouble exploiting you before you do it to me. In relationships that are not trustworthy, it is every person for himself or herself; dog-eat-dog.

The prospect of again experiencing such intense pain is what determines the way we will act in future relationships. At one extreme of this way of acting is controlling behavior; that is, if a relationship is not safe or trustworthy, then I will control all the risks involved with that relationship. If I cannot control the interactions, then I will not participate. This overcontrolling attitude is not the kind that is driven by a Type A perfectionistic attitude. Rather, it is an emotional response to our fear of being abused or neglected in relationships. For instance, the following statement was made by a man in his mid-30's concerning his wife. The couple had sought therapy because the man was overly controlling emotionally and was overly involved with his wife's health.

> "I just cannot let her alone. I think about her all the time. I have to make sure that she is going to take care of herself. I cannot risk her getting any sicker. I can barely manage our life on what we make together, and I don't know how we would manage if she stopped working. I also want to make sure that she still loves me and will not leave me. If I can't know or do something about it, I just about go crazy. Even at work, if one little thing goes wrong with an order or a delivery, I just can't handle it."

Although this man clearly did love his wife, he reduced his concern for her health to how it would affect him and the family financially. Further, his desire to make sure that she still loved him and would not leave was smothering the life and spontaneity out of the relationship. In this case, the man's father had deserted him and his sister after his mother was killed in an automobile accident. He was shifted from foster home to foster home and was never again able to relax in a secure environment. His solution for his insecurity was to try to actively control as many variables as possible.

People who become emotionally dependent on controlling relationships to protect themselves from pain may exhibit control in various ways. They may do it overtly by threatening physical, emotional, economic, or legal action in order to get the other person to "behave" in the way that is thought to be right. Such people are often seen as "little dictators" who bully other relational members into doing what they want them to do. Consider the threats of a young man to his wife who wanted to share more intimacy with him:

"I give you what I can give. If it is not enough, that's too bad. I'm not giving you the opportunity to know me inside and out just so you can use it against me. If you push me, we'll just skip to the end and divorce now."

This man, who had been emotionally manipulated by his mother while he was growing up, is clearly stating that the relationship will exist on his terms or not at all. He threatens divorce because his wife wants to know him emotionally. He assumes that if he loses part of himself to the intimacy of the relationship, his wife will use the information in an untrustworthy manner to do him harm.

But control in relationships can also be exercised in covert ways, such as by subtle manipulation or withdrawal. Some people who feel threatened in a relationship will distance themselves from the other person or refuse to reveal their thoughts. When things go amiss in the relationship, they seldom acknowledge their contribution to the problem, but instead wait for the other to take full responsibility. In this way, the controllers maintain the power over the relationship so it will not hurt them. But whether expressing their desire to control overtly or covertly, people who choose such action to deal with their pain do so to protect themselves from further exploitation.

Chaos. When we are violated in areas of trustworthiness, we may try to escape entering relationships in order to avoid future hurt. Instead of trying to control all the power in the relationship and make you obey my rules, I spend my time trying to escape your power and to avoid your rules. However, since I come from a legacy of pain, I may see any form of relationship as potentially damaging, so that even the most reasonable expectations become burdensome and threatening.

People who are driven by chaotic behavior have assumed the attitude that relationships are established to damage them and that it is just a matter of time before they will be hurt. There are few pleasures in life, so the best I can do is to try to maximize the good times. Therefore, if I have a choice of doing what is good for the relationship or of satisfying my own pleasure, I will satisfy my own pleasure. I will do so even if I am aware that my behavior will have severe long-range consequences, for in the end, bad consequences are going to catch up with me anyway. For example, consider the words of a young woman who was involved in an ongoing incestuous relationship with her father, after she left her husband and young son.

"I was at the bank and a man tried to pick me up. I didn't feel that attracted to him, but it was as if I thought: Here is my chance to get out. My husband will eventually find me out and my son will hate me; here is my chance to avoid that. So I left and stayed with the man for three days."

The woman was in a hurtful and damaging relationship with her father which caused her great pain, but she also had responsibilities in her relationship with her husband and son. But because facing the pain of confronting her father was too overwhelming, she chose a chaotic solution to avoid her discomfort even though she knew that the affair would cause even deeper problems.

People who indulge in chaotic behavior to avoid pain appear to be very irresponsible with regard to relationships. However, their behavior is not caused by a lack of maturity or by irresponsibility, but rather by hopelessness, by the assumption that they will experience pain in every relationship. To deal with this pain, they are driven to chaos in order to escape.

Although addictive behavior is associated with all four manifestations of pain, people driven by chaos are the most likely to engage in such behavior. Addictions often develop because individuals try to mitigate their pain by indulging in some type of addictive substance or behavior. Eventually, the substance or behavior becomes an essential part of maintaining life. People who deal with pain out of chaos are susceptible to choosing such methods for mitigating pain and then holding onto the addiction in spite of the consequences for their relationships. This was the case with a man in his mid-50's who chose alcohol over his relationship with his grandchildren.

> "I know what I am doing. I mean, I don't know whether or not I'm addicted to the booze. I don't care. But I do know that it is causing my children to not allow me to see the grandchildren. I think that they are right, and I think that it is best for everyone concerned. If I got to know those grandkids, they would just be telling me that I shouldn't drink and how I should be and how my drinking hurts them. That's what they would be doing eventually. This way, I can just avoid all that hassle."

Driven by intense pain, this man avoids any potential pain by proclaiming a deeper commitment to his alcoholism. This sense of pervasive hopelessness is seen most clearly in people driven by chaos who believe that life will "get" them in the end. Desertion, addiction, financial irresponsibility, and manipulation are the tools of the trade in this mode of functioning. Although chaos is driven by the lack of hope that relationships can be trustworthy and healthy, people driven by chaos may not look hopeless at all. Outwardly, they may appear jovial, carefree, and lighthearted. Inside, however, they carry the deep sense of violation that drives the erratic, and mostly irresponsible, behavior.

Control and Chaos Cycles. Are there *turn stylers* in dealing with the pain associated with violations of trustworthiness? The answer is "Yes," although I see fewer of these than of those who experience a rage/shame cycle. When it does exist, however, the behavior resembles that of a person with a bipolar affective disorder who at times has hyperactive and manic tendencies and then will have periods of depressed and hopeless behavior. However, with control/chaos turn stylers, the behavior will focus on trying to deal with the emotional pain that the person feels. People involved in these types of cycles will find themselves overcontrolling relationships, finances, and their personal lives, such as exercise regimes and health, trying to make sure that their "ducks are in a row" and feeling desperate and at risk when they are not powerful enough to keep things the way they believe they should be. As things become more unruly and out of line with expectations and power, they often will resign from all power and responsibility and "escape" into some type of indulgent behavior designed to calm their anxiety and pain. Such was the case with a mother of four who had grown up in a physically abusive home.

"I try all the time. I work all the time. I try to help my kids with school and to take care of them at home. I take care of all the bills. I'm always taking care of how everyone feels and getting them where they need to be. They don't appreciate it one bit. They're always telling me to butt out or leave them alone. When we don't have enough money, my husband blames me. So, I just finally get to the point where I don't care. I go out and buy new appliances or a new stereo. I'll go on a trip for a few days without telling anyone where I'm going. I almost always quit my job at that point. But then I get to the point where I feel too unstable and I go back. The whole process starts over."

Again, where these types of *turn stylers* exist, one extreme behavior does not balance the other. Both extremes are unhealthy and result in the victim's becoming extremely unstable and untrustworthy. Although controlling people are accepted because they are usually perfectionistic and attentive to details, such as paying bills on time and keeping emotions in check, in relationships they are overbearing and demanding of others while emotionally withholding themselves. Chaotic people are unstable and unpredictable in relationships and appear to use people or situations for what they can take and get. When the two are merged into a cycle, people around them are confused, frustrated, and damaged by the interactions.

Special Focus Three:
Understanding Your Style of Dealing
with Painful Violations

Directions: Rate the following statements as they apply to you. Because each person is unique, there are no right or wrong answers. Just try to respond as honestly as you can. Please respond to every statement.

After reading each statement, check the answer that BEST describes the way you feel or act.

1. People don't ask my advice or opinion.

___ Yes, I believe this is mostly true.
___ No, this is mostly false.

2. Nobody knows how I really feel.

___ Yes, I believe this mostly true.
___ No, I believe this is false.

3. I easily misplace things.

___ Yes, I do this much of the time.
___ No, this is rarely the case.

4. I am ashamed of what has happened to me.

___ Yes, I feel this much of the time.
___ No, I seldom feel this way.

5. I hit things when I am really angry.

___ Yes, this happens often.
___ No, this hardly ever happens.

6. Winning is very important to me.

___ Yes, I believe this is mostly true.
___ No, I rarely feel this way.

7. I can stay with tasks until they are complete.

___ Yes, I do this much of the time.
___ No, this is rarely the case.

8. I need to cover up how I really feel.

___ Yes, I feel this most of the time.
___ No, I seldom feel this way.

9. I feel like smashing things.

___ Yes, I feel this way often.
___ No, I seldom feel this way.

10. I swear a lot when I am mad.

___ Yes, I do this much of the time.
___ No, this hardly ever happens.

11. I don't want people to know what happened to me.

___ Yes, this is mostly true.
___ No, this is mostly false.

12. I have difficulty compromising with other people.

___ Yes, I believe this is mostly true.
___ No, this is seldom true.

13. I feel hopeless and alone.

___ Yes, this is mostly true.
___ No, this is mostly false.

14. It is often better to cover up your feelings.

___ Yes, I believe this is mostly true.
___ No, I seldom feel this way.

15. This person causes me to feel so angry, I cannot think.

___ Yes, this happens often.
___ No, this seldom happens.

16. I feel responsible for what this person did to me.

___ Yes, I feel this much of the time.
___ No, I seldom feel this way.

17. When in an argument, I have been known to throw things.

___ Yes, this happens often.
___ No, this hardly ever happens.

18. People say that I'm co-dependent.

___ Yes, I believe this is mostly true.
___ No, this does not happen.

19. After work or school, I have no motivation to get anything accomplished.

___ Yes, I believe this is mostly true.
___ No, I seldom feel this way.

20. Life feels organized.

___ Yes, I believe this is mostly true.
___ No, I seldom feel this way.

21. I feel enraged often.

___ Yes, this happens much of the time.
___ No, this seldom happens.

22. People say that I am a person who has to have my way.

___ Yes, I believe this is mostly true.
___ No, this is mostly false.

Scoring the Scale

The foregoing was taken from the *Pain Scale* of the *Interpersonal Relationship Resolution Scale* (Hargrave & Sells, 1997). The scale is designed to give you an idea of how you deal with violations of love and trust in terms of behavior that can be characterized in the constructs of *shame, rage, control,* and **chaos**.

Shame

Shame is the degree to which an individual internalizes painful or undesirable experiences. Shame is a global measure that assesses the overall manifestation of personal guilt. High scores (10 or above) may mean that the individual is comfortable with mild levels of confrontation and is secure with self. Low scores (8 or below) may indicate that individuals experience excessive guilt and internalize emotions that indicate the self is unacceptable.

Rage

Rage is the degree to which an individual externalizes painful or undesirable experiences. It is a global measure that assesses internal feelings of anger and actions that are manifestations of anger. High scores (10 or above) may indicate that the individual does not express anger in an overt manner. Low scores (9 or below) may indicate that the individual expresses anger and resentment in external ways.

Control

Control is the degree to which an individual seeks to lead his or her life in such a way as to avoid or deal with situations. It is a global measure that assesses overall efforts in managing life. High scores (7 or above) may reflect a relaxed style of conducting activities and relationships. Low scores (6 or below) may reflect an authoritarian style of dealing with life goals or relationships.

Chaos

Chaos is the degree to which an individual seeks to avoid organization or responsibility in dealing with situations. It is a global measure that assesses an overall failure to manage life successfully. High scores (11 or above) may reflect a balanced effort in organizing life goals and being considered responsible. Low scores (9 or below) may reflect an inability to organize and manage life goals and relationships.

Add the following together:

SHAME score

2.	1 for Yes, 2 for No	___
4.	1 for Yes, 2 for No	___
8.	1 for Yes, 2 for No	___
11.	1 for Yes, 2 for No	___
13.	1 for Yes, 2 for No	___
16.	1 for Yes, 2 for No	___
	TOTAL:	___

RAGE score

5.	1 for Yes, 2 for No	___
9.	1 for Yes, 2 for No	___
10.	1 for Yes, 2 for No	___
15.	1 for Yes, 2 for No	___
17.	1 for Yes, 2 for No	___
21.	1 for Yes, 2 for No	___
	TOTAL:	___

CONTROL score

6.	1 for Yes, 2 for No	___
12.	1 for Yes, 2 for No	___
14.	1 for Yes, 2 for No	___
22.	1 for Yes, 2 for No	___
	TOTAL:	___

CHAOS *score*

1.	1 for Yes, 2 for No	___
3.	1 for Yes, 2 for No	___
7.	2 for Yes, 1 for No	___
18.	1 for Yes, 2 for No	___
19.	1 for Yes, 2 for No	___
20.	2 for Yes, 1 for No	___
	TOTAL:	___

THE EFFECTS OF VIOLATIONS AND PAIN

Whether the violation is rooted in lack of love, lack of trustworthiness, or both, family acts that assault and insult us cause pain that affects us deeply. No matter how we deal with that pain internally, how we feel about ourselves (rage, shame, or both), and how we act in relationships (controlling, chaotic, or both), the ravages of the violations are evident in our lives.

As victims of family injustice and damage, we are likely to play out the damage in other relationships that are innocent, most likely with spouses, children, and close friends. The burden of abuse and damage that made us victims now motivates us, sometimes unconsciously, to damage others and victimize them. The abused now becomes the abuser. We hate ourselves for the acts we commit against others, overt and covert, but we feel entitled to our damaging behavior because of the damage that we have suffered.

Even when we stand up to the abuse and swear that we will never again repeat the evil acts that were perpetuated against us, we are internally programed to not being loved or not being in relationships that are trustworthy. For example, many will try to accumulate money or property to cover the pain and hurt. Some will change geographic locations, whereas others will doggedly pursue their careers. Still others will try to cover their pasts with better relationships. But people who try to forget their pasts by such means soon find that when they experience pain in current relationships, they escape by dedicating themselves to earning still more or trying to "buy" the relationships by threatening to withdraw financial support. People who escape into careers soon find that not only have they relinquished their past painful relationships, but also any possibility of being in other relationships.

New relationships may look safe, but soon a familiar prognosis of damage becomes evident. Men and women who escape domineering and manipulative parents through marriage will often find themselves with an even more domineering spouse whom they thought would be strong enough to "handle" the controlling parents. However, the person soon finds that the domineering spouse is more controlling or manipulative than the parents were. Or, the man or woman may marry an a overly irresponsible person whom the controlling parents hate. Soon, however, the person finds it impossible to deal with the irresponsibility of the new spouse, and has to take more and more control. He or she wakes up one day to find himself or herself dominating the spouse in the same way that he or she was once controlled, and comes to the painful realization that he or she has become just like his or her parents.

Nothing is sadder than when a person realizes that all the efforts that have been made to "do things differently" than the people who caused such damage have only guaranteed the same type of violation. Such was the case with a woman who came to therapy because of her inability to form a close relationship with her extremely needy and insecure partner. When the therapist inquired about the type of family she had grown up in, the woman became agitated and angry.

> "My mother divorced my father the year I was born, claiming that he wasn't a good provider. She worked all her life, and demanded the same type of work of me. She would never let me cry or express any sadness, she always said there was no room for weakness. She despises the type of person I am."

After hearing the story, the therapist asked permission to contact the mother to attempt to understand the daughter's perception. When asked about her own mother, the woman's mother also became agitated and angry.

> "My mother didn't care one bit for me. She lay around all day in bed whining because her life was so miserable. My father ran around with other women and all she would do was become depressed and go to bed. She never confronted him. She never did anything. She was pathetic. She didn't raise me; I had to take care of myself, and sometimes her. I swore that I would never be like her."

Indeed, she certainly wasn't like her own mother: a take-control woman who would never be weak and dependent, had provided well for herself and her daughter (the client), had raised the daughter in a "tough as nails" atmosphere that left her believing that she wasn't as important as her mother's work and that her weakness was unacceptable. Thus, although this mother's approach to the relationship was opposite to that of her own mother, in the end the results were the same. Her daughter felt the same lack of love and care from her as she had from her daughter's grandmother. The damage that had been done to her was perpetuated on others.

In essence, then, pain and hurt experienced in the family spawn a continual imbalance in the way we feel about ourselves and go about relational give-and-take. This imbalance drains love and trustworthiness from the family, and those of us who are affected feel justified in seeking our just entitlement in destructive ways. This destructive entitlement results in manipulation, dysfunctional family patterns, and in the worst cases, damage to the psyches of family members who feel the shame of not being loved. Although their cause and manifestations are obvious in cases of physical abuse, incest, or profound neglect, pain and hurt resulting from less "extreme" acts can be just as real. Lack of interest, manipulation, or substance addictions may be important sources of pain and hurt in the family, even though the destructive patterns may not seem violent. The key component is not the actual pattern or destructive act, but the drain on the family's resources of trust and love. Any act that consistently contributes to the deterioration of family love and trust will eventually result in hurt and pain.

Family pain and hurt may originate from the same sources — lack of love and deterioration of trustworthiness — but it is important to remember that they may differ in magnitude. Both the victim of manipulation by an alcoholic family member and the person victimized by severe physical abuse will feel insults to their personhoods and lose trust in their relationships, but the latter may feel greater pain because of the violence associated with the assault. Generally, the greater family pain accumulates as the severity and longevity of the destructive acts increase.

Pain can also be caused by outside factors, such as suffering a genetic accident or an incurable diseases, or experiencing a natural disaster. But it is only within the context of relationships that we have an expectation of love and trust. Therefore, relationships are unique in that people are held accountable for their actions concerning love and trust and are responsible for making the relationships right when there is something wrong or lacking. This is true of all relationships, but especially of family relationships.

It is in this framework of pain and violation that forgiveness is necessary. In some traditional psychological therapies, the goal is to change the way those who have been violated feel or behave. If a person feels shamed, the therapy tries instead to motivate feelings of rage toward the perpetrator of the violation. If a person has chaotic behavior, then the therapy directs more controlled behavior, or vice versa. Still other therapists seek to understand the past, hoping that talking about the acts will relieve the manifestations of the pain. Some victims will try their own methods of just doing *something* different in relationships, burying the past, and hoping that their future relationships will turn out better. However, when the justified balance of give-and-take is violated to the point that trust in the relationship has disappeared, or a person's entitled need to know that he or she is loved and wanted has been insulted, the resulting damage will affect every aspect of future relationships. Only by addressing the violation of love and trust is it possible to heal the psyches and actions of both victims and victimizers. The four stations of forgiveness are aimed at healing this damage by restoring the love, justice, and trust needed in relationships.

References

Boszormenyi-Nagy, I., & Krasner, B. (1986). *Between give and take: A clinical guide to contextual therapy.* New York: Brunner/ Mazel.

Hargrave, T. D. & Sells, J. N. (1997). The development of a forgiveness scale. *Journal of Marital and Family Therapy, 1,* 41–62.

Section Two

Maintaining the Work of Forgiveness:
The Four Stations

3

Station One:

Insight and Learning How to Stop Hurt

The work of forgiveness in families may seem magical and even mystical at times. Families, like mine, that were seriously dysfunctional to the point where even simple interactions were painful, and sometimes impossible, seem to be restored to a familiar and longed-for health. Consider the woman who now sits laughing and talking about old family vacations with her arm around the father who once sexually abused her. Or the man who gladly allows his parents to take his children on a weekend trip even though he himself had been severely physically abused by the parents 20 years earlier. The work of forgiveness in relationships is that of reestablishing love and trust in relationships, and when that has been accomplished, it can have an enormously healing effect on even the most damaged of relationships. But the process is neither magical nor mystical. Not every relationship will undergo such a complete transition, but they all can have an element of forgiveness. In forgiving the "devils" of your past, it is necessary to start down a difficult and, at times, shadowed road. There are several points of demarcation, however, that can make the road clearer and easier to travel.

The first point of demarcation in making the journey of forgiveness clearer is the station of *insight*. Insight is a method of salvage that allows people to take actions that are designed to put an end to hurtful interactions and to take initial steps toward building trust. This is where all forgiveness must begin. If I am rowing a boat across a deep lake, and a diver comes up under my boat with a sharp instrument and drives a hole in the vessel, my first thought after plugging the hole is how to protect myself from the diver's doing the same thing again. It will be impossible to trust the diver or to develop any kind of relationship if I cannot be relatively sure that I am protected against similar future damage.

Forgiveness is not just about showing love for the people who damaged us. Love does have a place in forgiveness, but it is not the whole story. To forgive someone out of love while he or she continues to damage us makes us appear weak. This type of forgiveness just sets us up to be damaged all over again. It also does the victimizer no good because it does not cause him or her to take responsibility and change his or her behavior. In order for forgiveness to really be forgiveness, it must include the kindness of love, the trustworthiness and responsibility of justice, and the power to protect and change. Forgiveness without justice or power keeps us victims.

Insight is about gaining power in a relationship that has damaged you. The priority at this station of forgiveness is to minimize the risk of further relational injury. Insight allows a person to see the interactions and mechanisms that have caused the damage and hurt and, in turn, this perspective provides him or her with the means to protect himself or herself from further hurt and damage.

INSIGHT

All pain and wrongs are the result of some type of interaction. Sometimes actions are covert, as when you pick up someone's disapproval of you or your actions even though that person does not say a word. Sometimes the actions are overt, as in yelling, beating, or inappropriate touching. But all violations of love and trust are perpetuated within the context of real actions. Insight is the station of forgiveness that allows us to objectify the real actions or the mechanisms of pain that have caused the relational damage. Once we identify those actions and mechanisms, we can learn to stop or block the relational damage from occurring in the future. In this manner, we do not restore trust to a relationship that has been damaging per se, but we set the stage for trust to be built because we have stopped the damage. Insight has limited ability to *heal* relationships, but it does help us to put the brakes on additional relational damage.

Most often, however, it is not so easy to identify exactly what the transactions are that cause us damage and distress. It is like opening a refrigerator that contains a bad apple or spoiled onion. We know that something is wrong, but it is not easy to tell the good from the bad. All we know is that something smells awful. The fault is not in our senses. The fault lies in our inability to locate the source of the problem. Likewise, when we experience severe relational injustices and wrongs, our emotions clearly tell us that something is wrong. We feel used, abused, manipulated, and cheated, but these feelings do not necessarily direct us to the real problem or to identify how the hurt was perpetuated on us.

Step One: Identifying the Heart of the Violation

The first step in insight is clearly to identify the heart of the violation, or what wrong was done to us in the relationship. This may sound easy, but when we are dealing with family members or relationships with whom or in which we have long histories of hurt, it can become confusing. Because of the pain, we often have trouble articulating exactly what the violation of trust was or how we knew that we were not loved. This is seen in the story told by an adult son whose stepmother had treated him and his sister with total disregard.

> "I can tell you why I hate her. She has no interest in my children at all or in my life. When I have to go see her, all she talks about is her latest sickness or how she is doing. She is totally wrapped up in herself."

He probably does hate the fact that his stepmother does not take any interest in his children or in him, but it is doubtful that this lack of interest would be enough to cause him to hate her. What is the source for such hate? Most likely, it is the step-mother's lack of love for the man and his sister when they were children and needed that love and trustworthy care the most. The current interactions among him, his children, and his stepmother are not the cause of the hate, but a result of her selfishness when he was younger. Even if she were to show interest in the man's children, he still would probably bear ill will toward her. In order to have the interaction make a difference, the adult son would have to clearly identify the source of the violation: his step-mother's lack of care and nurture for him when he was younger.

It can be helpful to victims of relational abuse to have them summarize the transgression in a global statement about the status of love and trust in the relationship. For instance, the man above could sum up his emotional turmoil concerning his stepmother with a statement such as, "I could not trust her to take care of me and my sister," or "She cannot be trusted because she would only look out for herself." These types of statements about the status of violation in the areas of love and trust help us to identify the source of our emotional turmoil. It then becomes easier to identi-fy specific examples that illustrate how we were not loved or why the relationship was not trustworthy. If we try to identify specific examples first, without identifying the powerful sense of violation of love and trust that causes the emotional turmoil, we may find it difficult to justify our feelings. This was the case with an adult woman who had trouble justifying her sense of violation by her alcoholic mother.

> "I feel so hurt and angry when I call her and she is drunk. She tells me that she is not hurting anyone because she lives by herself and that I have no right to get upset. Sometimes I think she is right, but then I feel this terrible pit in my stomach."

The woman feels terrible because the drinking is a reminder of the mother's alcoholism when she was younger. The mother, while doing many things right, left the daughter with a feeling of insecurity, of not knowing when her mother was going to be reliable and when she was not. Therefore, the daughter still feels that ache of lack of reliability and trust in the relationship but is unable to express it clearly because she starts with the current interaction with the mother.

Insight into the source of the relational damage allows us to clarify the emotional turmoil we may feel. This turmoil does not have to be proved or justified, nor can it be dismissed or denied. The insight, in turn, provides the victim with confidence in knowing that a violation did occur in the relationship and that there actually is a problem. Knowing where the violation occurred validates the emotions that may arise (rage, shame, control, chaos) because it correctly identifies the origin of the damage.

Step Two: Keeping the Violation Where It Belongs

Insight into the violation also provides us with the ability to place the violation, and the corresponding emotions, with the person who was responsible for the violation. If I were punished by being locked in a closet for days at a time when I was young, I am likely to remain untrusting, fearful, or enraged. If, however, I do not have the insight to place the responsibility with the one who violated me, I am likely to be untrusting, fearful, or enraged in any relationship, including those with my spouse, children, friends, or employers. Insight assists us in clarifying our emotional reactions to relationships and confining them to the relationships where they originated to ensure that they do not poison subsequent relationships.

In the previous chapter, we have discussed how the interactions and violations of one generation can set up the next one to make similar mistakes. Because you were denied what you deserved from a relationship and were the victim of an unjust hurt, you are a candidate to take more than you deserve from another relationship and so violate an innocent person. For example, if I feel unloved because my parents never expressed love to me and expected me to provide security for them, I may feel justified in manipulating my children and holding them responsible for providing love and security for me. We all find ourselves repeating harmful actions or phrases that we once considered damaging. Even though I may truly hate to hurt other people, I may feel entitled to get what I "deserve" because of the way I was hurt by others. In this way "the beat goes on," and family damage and the resulting pain are perpetuated. This is seen in the following statement by a mother in her mid-40's who provided little care for her daughters because of her depression.

> "I have always had to take care of someone; my mother, her husband, my siblings. I've been ignored and abused for 40 years. It is my turn to be taken care of. They [the daughters] have just got to understand that it is their job to take care of me for awhile."

When insight is gained, it clarifies the relational issues, such as who is responsible for the damage and why we feel the turmoil we feel. But insight also provides us with the ability to realize that we are potential victimizers and that the violation that was perpetuated on us does not justify irresponsible or unloving actions to others.

Step Three: Identifying and Changing the Current Actions That Cause Pain

All relationships have "rules" or ways that govern how they function. Some of these rules focus on the issue of leadership and hierarchy, such as who is in charge and makes the decisions in the relationship. Another issue of hierarchy may relate to which members are expected to carry out the leader's demands. Another way in which these rules surface is in traditional beliefs, such as "adults know best" or "children are to be seen and not heard." And relationships also have rules concerning the interactions that take place. In many relationships, the rules require that all communication and thoughts must be open to the participants. Other relationships mandate just the opposite: all thoughts must be kept secret.

Some relationships have rules and patterns of interacting that are deeply dysfunctional. In many of these dysfunctional relationships, members engage in repeated actions that cause relational damage. For instance, two spouses may not be able to tolerate the emotional closeness of an intimate relationship. Any interaction between the two results in turmoil. In order to handle necessary communications such as time schedules, responsibilities, or finances, they may covertly agree to delegate the task to a child. "Tell your father that I want him to take out the trash." "Doesn't your mother know that we can't afford that?" These types of statements represent co-opting a child into a dysfunctional pattern that not only will not help the spouses communicate, but will place an undue burden on the child. The result will be family rules that will cause relational damage.

All relational damage — whether by subtle manipulation, as in the example above, or by overt action, such as sexual abuse — has a dysfunctional pattern that communicates the damage to us. In other words, we experience hurt or pain from some actions in our relationships with people. It is these very patterns that continue to perpetuate the hurt to us. For instance, an incestuous family often has "rules" or a power structure which will not allow a violated child to confront or protect himself or herself from the abusing parent. Beliefs about loyalty, respect, or even fears concerning parents may result in damaging secrets or rules about behavior long after the child has grown into an adult. The abusing parent may continue to feel the power to say or do sexually inappropriate things to the adult son or daughter, and the family structure and belief system may be such that the behavior has to be tolerated. This was the case with a woman who felt the pain of sexual abuse every time she visited her parents' home.

"I was fondled by my father a lot between the ages of 8 and 13. My mother knew it, but never did anything to protect me. I used to try to avoid him, but he would manage to get me alone in my room almost every week. I had no escape. When I go see them now, he always wants to grab me before I leave, kiss me on the mouth or try to give me a hard hug. It feels awful, like he is doing the same thing to me that he was when I was young. I just want to escape, but I can't figure out what to say or what to do."

The truth about this situation is that the father is still doing inappropriate things with the adult daughter and is using the same dysfunctional "rules" in the family to maintain his damaging behavior. The daughter feels trapped because the family rules have not changed to allow her to confront the situation. These rules and the family organization allow her to be abused over and over again and remind her of the past incest. *The organization and rules of the family that allowed the damaging transaction to occur in the first place will allow the damage to reoccur in the future.* In this way, relational transactions often perpetuate the pain of a victim, even though no future violation may take place. We rightly feel at risk in a system or relationship where we have been hurt before and where nothing has changed.

The most important work of insight lies in being able to identify the damaging transactions and rules that have caused us pain and hurt, and then to change the relational interaction so that we cannot be hurt again. The identification of patterns, communication, and relational rules gives us, who have been hurt unjustly, the ability to avoid or stop harmful or painful patterns and to break rules that cause additional hurt. For instance, an only daughter who, as an adult, was having trouble forming any significant intimate relationship sought therapy because she could not trust any partner or friend. When she started discussing the family in which she had grown up, it became clear that her parents had used her to try to take care of their relationship. Instead of talking directly to each other about their desires or problems, each would tell the daughter, and she would then be responsible for convincing the other to make changes. When asked if she visited her parents often, she said "Yes," and told the following story:

"It is the same thing every time I go to see them. I walk in and go up the stairs with my mother right behind me. While I'm unpacking, she will sit on the bed and tell me everything horrible that my father is or has been doing. It's the same thing with my father. Sometime during my visit, he will get me alone or take me along on an errand and he will tell me everything horrible about my mother. I hate visiting them."

When asked why she visited if she hated the transaction, she reported that she felt responsible for her parents' happiness since they had been so good to her as an only child. She knew how they depended on her and believed that they really loved her.

It is clear that the "rules" in this family were that since the parents could not tolerate speaking directly to each other, they could depend on the daughter to handle their problems. Also, however, there were family rules that demanded that the daughter be loyal to the parents because they were good to her financially or were loving people. But the rules made it impossible for the daughter to be free to pursue her own relationships because she felt so responsible for her parents' relationship. She was the victim of an untrustworthy manipulation that continued to damage her ability to pursue potentially healthy relationships.

After the daughter clearly identified that the parents were using her in an untrustworthy way and that they should take responsibility for their own relationship, she began to examine the transactions in the family and how she could change her behavior in such a way as to end the manipulation. After detailing how she was caught up in the interaction, she came up with the following solution, which she reported on her next visit:

"I went home to visit and, true to form, as I went upstairs, my mother followed. As I started unpacking, she started the litany against my father. Instead of listening, I asked her to hold on a minute and I went downstairs and got my father. I sat him down on the bed and told him what Mom had said so far, and then asked her to continue. She stumbled around a bit as I unpacked. Needless to say, my father didn't try to get me alone to complain about my mother."

Changing the interaction for this woman meant that she communicated very directly to the parents that she would no longer carry their secrets or be responsible for changing one parent to please the other. The parents now must choose to either face one another or keep silent in the daughter's presence. This change in the family "rules" or transactions allows the daughter to move away from her parents' relationship and toward her own. In short, the changed family interaction allows her to be freed from her parents' manipulation and any further relational violations of trustworthiness.

Consider another example from the adult woman who had been sexually abused by her father and continued to feel awful every time she visited her parents. After identifying that the behavior of her father and mother was a clear violation of love and trust, she became willing to say to herself that what the father did to her was wrong. She then began to examine the family rules that continued to leave her open to victimization by the father. She stated:

"It is in the secret that he is powerful. As long as he is able to hide behind the disguise of being a loving and affectionate parent, he can continue to do whatever he wants to me. I've got to let the secret out in the open."

Her solution to the damaging transaction was to tell her family that she had been sexually abused by her father. Her husband and her sons responded with support for her and told her that they would not allow her father to act inappropriately again without calling him on his actions. She then told her father that she remembered the sexual abuse and how wrong it was. Although he denied doing anything wrong with her, saying that it was just his way of showing his love, she remained steadfast in her position.

She continued by saying that any time the father hugged or kissed her, or said anything inappropriate, she would tell him in front of everybody that his actions reminded her of how he sexually abused her when she was a little girl. Two weeks later, the woman had the following story:

> "I visited him and Mom last week, and as I was about to leave, he came toward me to give me a front hug and a kiss. Just before he got me, I raised my hand and said that he couldn't do that stuff to me anymore. If he wanted to get sex, I told him, he should go to his wife. I turned around and left. I feel he can't ever get to me again."

Once we identify the interactions that cause us pain and take actions to change them, then we have the power to protect ourselves. This power, gained through insight, allows us to make sure that no future damage will be inflicted on us. We may not be able to change our being a victim of manipulation or abuse in the past, but when we change the current interactions in relationships around us, we can prevent our becoming victims in the future.

Generally, the better you are able to articulate how dysfunctional family patterns contributed to your pain, the better you will be able to guard yourself against being hurt in the future. It is good to practice the damaging interactions before you participate in them to find the exact place where you feel violated or manipulated. Trust your feelings to tell you when something is being done that is wrong. It is usually reminding you of some pattern in the family that is, or has been, damaging.

When I help a person delineate the rules or interactions that were hurtful to him or her, I usually ask the person to describe the last situation that was painful. I ask what he or she did, and I write the answer down. I then ask what happened next in response to his or her actions, and again I write it down. I ask how he or she responded to this response, and continue the process until there is a list of interactions that are clearly detailed. Then I ask the person to identify the feelings associated with the interaction and what he or she would like to change about that feeling. We discuss the possibility of changing the interaction in a way that could bring about the desired feeling. You can see how this clarifies the interactions and rules in relationships from the following dialog between myself and a young man who sought therapy and who was overly controlled by his father with regard to his college and career decisions.

THERAPIST: Tell me about your last discussion.

SON: I wanted to tell him that I was thinking about changing my major from accounting to history, but I couldn't get it out of my mouth.

THERAPIST: So, what did you get out?

SON: I asked him what he thought about me and accounting.

THERAPIST: What was his response?

SON: He told me that I would do well financially in an accounting career, and that he didn't want me to struggle the way he always had. He said I would be a good provider if I had that degree.

THERAPIST: What did you say?

SON: I wanted to say that I hated accounting and was failing, but ended up just nodding okay.

THERAPIST: How did he respond?

SON: He kind of gave me this pep talk about how I could do anything I wanted and how proud we all would be when I finished.

THERAPIST: And you?

SON: I just gave up. I just was silent.

THERAPIST: How did you feel?

SON: Hopeless. There is no way that I can get through accounting and no way I can tell him I want to change. He would go ballistic because he believes that I'm the great hope of the family.

THERAPIST: How would you like to feel about your father?

SON: I would like to feel like I could make my own

decisions about my future. I would like to feel like I wasn't responsible for making him happy with me. I wish I could talk with him.

The power structure of this family was such that it required him to be absolutely subordinate to his father's hopes and desires for him. The father (who had his own painful issues in his family) was controlling and manipulating the son's life in ways that left the son insecure about whether the father loved him and whether he would ever be allowed to grow up.

The son and I talked about the possibilities of changing the interactions between him and his father so that he would not feel so dominated and controlled by his father's expectations and desires.

From the foregoing interaction, it is clear that the son gives up all of his control in the conversation from the beginning by following the same rules of the family ("What do *you* think about me and accounting?"). The son, by the way he starts the interaction, gives control and dominance to the father. I asked the young man to decide that he would seek to control his own thoughts in directing the conversation and not subjugate them to what his father was thinking. I then directed the son to think of some things that he could say that would be direct and would keep him in control.

THERAPIST:	Have you thought of something? Say it as though I were your father.
SON:	I could say, "I want to tell you some of my thoughts about accounting."
THERAPIST:	Go on.
SON:	"I don't believe accounting is a good fit for me. I do believe I need a degree, but I think I need to find another field."
THERAPIST:	(*acting like father*) "You will do as I say. I didn't pay for you to go to school to play around. You are good at accounting, and you will do what I want."

At this point, the young man hesitated and became lost. It was clear that he could feel the pressure that his father would exert on him if he stood up and tried to take control. This is the critical point of interaction to determine whether the son would acquiesce to his father and once again feel hopeless, or whether he would stand up and take control of his own life and stop the father's manipulation. A common method that I suggest to change the interaction in cases where there are rules of interaction from a defensive or controlling person is to ask that person how he or she would respond if someone else were saying what they were saying. In other words, at this point in the conversation I directed the son to ask the father how he would respond if his own father had made that type of statement to him.

SON: "If your father said that to you, what would you say?"

THERAPIST: (*acting like the father*) "My father was long gone. He would never have cared."

SON: "But what would you say if he had said it to you?"

THERAPIST: "I would have told him that it was my life and that I had to live it the way I saw fit."

SON: (*after a long pause*) "That is what I have to say now. I have to live my own life."

THERAPIST: (*after a pause and now acting as self*) How does that feel?

SON: Better. Tough, but better. I think I could do this.

The son did have a very similar conversation with his father a week later. However, he started by asking his father how he would feel if someone was always telling him what to do and how to live his life. The father responded in a defiant manner, which gave the son the strength and confidence to stand up to his father's controlling manipulation. A long and serious discussion about the son's options and the father's involvement, in terms of both financial commitment and advice giving, ensued. The son did switch majors and began to work part-time to pay toward his degree. However, the power alignment between the son and father shifted significantly, and the son never again felt helpless to resist his father's will.

Often, the people or situations that damaged us are long gone. For instance, a father or mother who was responsible for sexual abuse has been dead for 10 years. Perhaps you have cut off all communication with parents who were physically abusive and you have no idea where they are. In these situations, it is still profitable and possible to learn different interactions to prevent damaging transactions. It is done in much the same manner as above, but the interactions that are dealt with are ones that are remembered as significant by the victim. The same identification of feelings and the same goal of changing the interactions are discussed; however, the process of changing the interaction is limited to either the role play with another person or therapist or the thought processes of the victim. For example, a woman who had been sexually abused by her father, who is now dead, reported feeling powerless to stand up for herself and not let others take advantage of her in current relationships.

THERAPIST: Go back to an instance where you remember that your father abused you. What would happen?

WOMAN: Almost the same every time. He would come into my room late at night, hold his hand over my mouth, and then abuse me.

THERAPIST: Now close your eyes and go back to a time that he abused you. Feel yourself in your bed and feel his hand over your mouth. Do you see it? (*Woman nods her head.*) Now see yourself as an adult walking through the door and catching your father abusing this little girl who is you. What is it you say?

WOMAN: (*Very strongly.*) I tell him that he is through abusing anybody. I tell him to get out of the room and leave this little girl alone or I'll call the cops. I jerk his hand away and scream!

THERAPIST: And what do you do for the little girl?
WOMAN: What I would do is hold her, tell her that I would
            protect her.

The woman clearly identified a change in the interaction that would allow her, as a grown woman, to stop her father from abusing a child. This identification gave her the power she needed to change the interaction. Once she took this position of power in her mind, it convinced her that she could be different in interactions in current relationships in which she felt powerless. In this way, insight helped the woman to become more willing to take care of herself and to be more assertive in relationships. Many people can use this type of insight to change the rules of past relationships that no longer concern them, but do affect the way in which they deal with current relationships. Insight, therefore, can be an extremely helpful way to pursue forgiveness for those who have been victimized by people who have died or who are still too dangerous to be in a relationship.

Step Three: Gain Insight Into the Truth About Yourself

As we have discussed before, we learn about who and what we are in the framework of relationships. Even the way we look or our general health is unknown to us until we "try it out" in our family relationships and environment. It is in these interactions that we internalize beliefs about what is true about our personhood and how others perceive us. If I grow up being controlled and manipulated, then I will unlikely feel competent to control myself and to be responsible for satisfying the wishes of someone else. If I am beaten or used for someone's perverse sexual pleasure, then I am likely to feel worthless and without value, except when people can use me. No matter what the family violation is, victims usually translate the pain, at some level, into a "belief" about themselves.

Insight into the truth about yourself is difficult to achieve because those who are the most powerful teachers of these lessons, members of your family, have taught you a lie. As a human being, you are precious and worthy. You are deserving of care and nurture. You are unique and capable of giving good "gifts" to others. If you are abused, however, you will feel just the opposite. In Western societies during this past century, we have placed a great emphasis on the worth and value of the individual. We have emphasized this perspective in our culture and government, and in expression. But even in societies that are more group-oriented, each individual is valued as making a valued contribution to the whole. Human beings are complex and wonderfully constructed with regard to both their attitudes and actions. This is the truth that makes us precious, worthy, deserving of care and nurture, and unique in our individuality and gifts. Insight does provide a basic framework that we all have value and worth just by virtue of our being humans. However, it must be noted that beliefs about one's self are not just based on the fact that something is said to be; they are based on our familial relationships and what those relationships have taught us about ourselves. Although change in one's internal psyche is possible, it is difficult to achieve through insight alone. Since we originally learn about ourselves in the context of family relationships, it is often those very relationships that we must call upon to modify those beliefs.

Nevertheless, insight is a necessary part of learning the truth about ourselves. It also offers us the ability to understand the forces and family relationships that shaped our personalities. If I was neglected as a child and learned that relationships were not trustworthy and that I could only depend on myself, as an adult I will probably approach relationships with a defensive and withholding attitude. Through insight, however, I can recognize that I do not have to respond to the forces that shaped my early experiences by withholding my trust from every relationship. Insight can help me acknowledge the internal conflicts that developed as a result of the past and show me how to move past those limitations in present relationships. Such was the case with a middle-aged woman who had been having difficulties in her relationship with her husband.

"My father committed suicide when I was a girl. My mother never trusted any person after that, and she was fairly cold and distant with me as well. I always wanted somebody to love me and felt desperately alone and frightened. But every time someone would get close, I would pull away. I'm scared when I'm away from my husband and scared when he gets close. I know that I have to start telling myself that my husband is safe and stop just responding to him out of fear."

Insight can give us the ability to raise to the conscious level those forces, relationships, and interactions that taught us the "lies," the destructive, harmful, and self-defeating messages we have come to believe. Through insight, we can disengage from these forces in our past and allow ourselves to see the "truth" and to make different choices about ourselves. In addition, it allows us to see how our damaged past influences our feelings and actions in current relationships and to make the necessary adjustments. This helps us to set boundaries with regard to how we will use relationships to meet our needs for love, acceptance, and pleasure.

INSIGHT AND THE WORK OF FORGIVENESS

The fact is that there are limits on how far insight can go in restoring love and trust to a relationship. What it can do is give us an honest perspective on the family violation, help us to recognize destructive situations so we can protect ourselves, and allow us to believe that we are worthy and valued individuals despite harmful actions taken against us, but it does not heal our sense of injustice or the pain we feel from the loss of trust and love. So how does insight help us with the process of forgiveness?

First, insight allows us to pinpoint the real cause of the violations and to learn how to protect ourselves from the future damage those relationships can cause. As discussed before, if we are ever to be able to trust someone who has previously victimized us, we must be reasonably assured that this person cannot damage us again in the same way. Insight into how the rules and interactions of the relationship have left us vulnerable to damage and then insight on how to change those hurtful interactions provide an initial step in our journey.

Second, when we recognize the interactions and rules that cause us hurt and pain, we are better able to see how our own rules and interactions in relationships cause pain to others. Likewise, when we learn how to stop the interactions that hurt us, we learn how to stop the way we interact that hurts others. When we stop our own destructive behavior through insight, we assure the next generation a more balanced view of love and trust. The next generation, in turn, will do better in incorporating love and trust into their relationships. In this way, insight can provide each generation with a better opportunity to go beyond the damage and violation to more love and trust. Past abuse, manipulation, and destruction are gradually dissipated as each generation does better at living and loving.

Finally, insight is sometimes the only work of forgiveness that we can do. Sometimes the people who hurt us are still unsafe and we can ill afford to make ourselves vulnerable to them. Even if I am totally cut off from the person who caused me damage, either because he or she has died or is too dangerous, I utilize insight to help make my life better and my current relationships healthier. When someone experiences or witnesses such violations as suicides, murders, and torture, insight allows that person to go on with life and deal with the reality of the pain, recognize how and why the violation was perpetrated, and stop it from happening again.

Special Focus Four:
Gaining Insight Into the Relationship

1. Try to identify one or a few situations that are examples of how you were victimized.

2. Are these situations examples of violations of love, of trust, or of both?

3. How did these situations make you feel? (For example: Worthless? Abused? Neglected? Fearful? Hopeless?)

4. Knowing that you were violated, how would you now like to feel in the presence of the victimizer?

5. Detail the interactional sequence in the above situations. (What did you do or say first? How did your victimizer respond? What did you do next?)

6. What could *you* do in the sequence of interactions that would have changed the outcome so that you might feel more like you wanted to feel? (If you have trouble thinking of possibilities, ask someone to help you.)

7. Roleplay the changed interaction with another person whom you trust or play out the changed interaction in your mind. If you roleplay, be sure to listen to the constructive feedback from the person trying to help you.

4

Station Two:

Understanding and Learning What Our Abuse Is About

Here is the story of an older father who was accused by his son of being absent from the family and passive while the mother was abusive to the children.

> "It's true. I wasn't around and as active as I should have been. It was a bad time for me. I came back from the war a different person. I saw many of my friends killed; I even did some killing myself. My best friend had his legs blown off right in front of me. I came back and I was a little crazy. I guess I was depressed. There were times that were so bad for me that I didn't know whether I was going to kill myself or kill all of you [the family]. So I withdrew. It was wrong, but I was afraid of what I might do to all of you. I withdrew."

Damage caused to us through either abuse or neglect is the result of irresponsible actions in the past of our victimizers, but that does not mean that the abuse was without reason. As in the story above, the man's passivity and withdrawal that his son considered irresponsible neglect were seen by the father as preferable to his committing suicide or murder. Thus, the action I consider unreasonable, irresponsible, and irrational may actually be well intended by the victimizer.

Most of the damage that happens as a result of relationships is similar to that above. There were reasons and circumstances that caused the actions that hurt us deeply. Even though they may seem unreasonable to us, these circumstances shaped the behavior of the people who violated us. If we are to salvage as much forgiveness as possible to improve ourselves and make ourselves better in relationships, then we must go on to the second station of forgiveness. We must seek to understand the circumstances and situations that influenced the people who caused us pain.

WHY WE SHOULD SEEK UNDERSTANDING

Insight allows us to see the mechanisms and actions that caused us pain and gives us the ability to stop future actions that will cause us further abuse. In short, it affords us the capability to see *how* damage occurred in a relationship so that we can avoid damage in the future. Understanding is different in that it gives us the ability to see *why* the injustices, damage, and abuse occurred.

When we have been abused and hurt in a relationship, the question of "why" always remains. Why was I not loved? Why would a family that was supposed to treat me well treat me so badly? Why did this person do such a thing to me? Such questions inspire us to try to find answers that will justify the abuse. This often leads us to what we consider justifiable responses, such as extreme rage against our abuser or extreme shame toward ourselves, as discussed in the previous chapter. The aim of understanding is to get at these questions of "why" and, in finding the answers, alleviate some of the pain that we experienced as a result of the wrongs done to us.

Guilt and Culpability

The injustices and damage that we have undergone must first

clearly be identified as being wrong. When a young woman is forced to perform sexual acts with men while her father photographs her, that clearly is a violation of the daughter's rights and is wrong. The father is undeniably guilty. When a young man and woman, fearful of their families and of the responsibility of caring for their newborn child, abandon the child on the street, the couple is guilty of violating what is right. When I speak of guilt, I do not mean it as an expression of the way we feel. Guilt is a burden that I bear when I do wrong. It is a brand that I wear that clearly proclaims that I am responsible for the wrong done and the consequences that result. As one of my professors, John Drakeford, used to say, "You do not *feel* guilty; you *are* guilty."

Culpability is related to guilt in that it deals with the factor of responsibility or blameworthiness of the victimizer. However, culpability takes into account the factors or influences that may mitigate some of the blame the perpetrator should bear. For instance, say two young men get into a fight because one hits the other at a sporting event and then proceeds to lash out at him verbally. The youth receiving the hit and abuse, desperate for escape, grabs a rock and hits the other youth on the head, causing his death. He is responsible for, or guilty of, causing the other's death. He is responsible for the wrong done. However, there is a limit on his culpability because the dead youth's actions were also wrong and this fact mitigates the amount of culpability the survivor must bear. There was a *reason* for him to take such action. This limit of culpability does not justify his actions or exonerate him from responsibility, but it does serve to limit the amount of blame that is appropriate.

It is possible that the person who hurt us is completely guilty and fully culpable. However, it may also be true that the guilty person is only partially culpable. Often, when a person is guilty of hurting us, we hold him or her culpable because we internalize the action into a self-injury. To be victimized often means that we feel the action has made us dirty, unworthy, worthless, and undeserving. As a result, those of us who have been victimized not only consider the victimizer culpable, but hold him or her responsible *for the way the person made us feel*. When we view a person's culpability through the lenses of how the action made us feel, it makes it difficult to see any circumstances that may have contributed to the abuse, and we can become enraged or shamed.

Rage and shame can be an overwhelming burden to bear when we have been unjustly harmed. When we identify a person as being totally guilty and culpable, we hold him or her responsible for disregarding us. When we are driven by these deep emotions, we often disdain or hate the one who has wronged us, or we harbor hate and disregard for ourselves. But when the rage and shame are left alone to fester, they in essence separate us from the real person, who is our victimizer, and the real people, who are ourselves. We come to believe that the one who abused us is an evil monster or that we ourselves are undeserving or inhuman worms. For instance, consider the words of a woman who was sold into prostitution by her father.

> "He is evil, bad to the core. There is not one thing about him that is human. He is just like a shark who has ripped pieces of me off, but he didn't quite kill me. The only way I could ever deal with him would be to kill him."

In the same conversation, the woman expresses some of how she sees her own value and worth.

> "I'm not much of a mother or wife. In fact, I'm really not much of anything. I've become so much of what my father sold me to be. [long pause] Sometimes, I think that he did what he did to me because he sensed that all I was from the very beginning was a whore and he just wanted to get his cut. That's all I am or ever have been ... a no-good whore. I don't deserve to be a mother or have anyone around me at all."

As I have said before, people are not monsters and we as humans are precious and worthy. Rage and shame put us out of touch with who we are and the humanity of others. Humans are indeed capable of evil and unjustified acts, but no human is beyond reason or, more important, beyond responsibility. When we continue to ask "why" and to look for guilt and culpability, we continue to hold a real *person* responsible for the hurt we have suffered. The desire to understand why someone would harm an innocent person is the effort to hold the victimizer accountable and responsible for his or her actions. This is true for all humans, but is especially important when the people who abused or violated us are family members. Station two in the work of forgiveness, *understanding*, gives us the ability to look at the guilt of the person who did us wrong and to make realistic determinations concerning his or her culpability for the violation.

Understanding Completes the Work of Salvage

When understanding and insight are coupled, we are able to accomplish *salvage* in the work of forgiveness. Salvage work in insight gives us the ability to protect ourselves and innocent parties from further relational damage. Salvage work in understanding gives us the ability to see the circumstances of the person who caused us the unjustified damage so that we can hold him or her responsible and free ourselves from the pain. When we do this work of salvage, we are not proclaiming the person as trustworthy for the future. Indeed, those who have violated us in the past may be just as destructive as ever. However, as we gain insight, the wrongdoer becomes less powerful because we are able to prevent the destructive situations from occurring again. Also, when we gain understanding, we are not excusing the person from responsibility for the action. Undeserved and unjustified actions remain undeserved and unjustified. When we seek understanding, we are determining how much culpability should be assigned to the violator so that we can assess the level of responsibility, and deal with the pain the action caused, as we think about ourselves. The station of understanding means that we come to understand and appreciate our abuser's situation, options, efforts, and limits, and see our own fallibility in dealing with such circumstances.

Understanding, therefore, leads us to a position where we do not have to condemn the victimizer, but we do hold them responsible. As we achieve understanding and attain a perspective on the real humans and the real responsibility, we have the potential of resolving some of the internalized pain resulting from the past injustices. True understanding causes pain to fade. When we understand, we come to know that neither the victim nor the victimizer is evil, but that the situations and the limits of both contributed to the inflicting of an unjustified wound in a real and fragile person. This does not make the relationship loving or trustworthy, but it does allow us to put our pain in perspective and to make it easier to live with ourselves, while others around us experience us as easier to live with.

As a victim, if you are going to be able to do the work of salvage in forgiveness and move on with your life, you must learn to master past injustices with *power* and *identification*. Insight should give you the power to stop the injustice. But preventing future relational injustices is only part of the work of salvage. Complete salvage also involves understanding the victimizer so that you can also understand the whys of the violation. Identification is the key element at work in the second station of forgiveness, *understanding*.

UNDERSTANDING

It is sometimes a difficult concept to explain to abused people, but the fact is that we all deserve nurture, care, respect, and love in relationships. It is fair for those to whom we relate to expect these things from us, and it is fair for us to expect these things from them. We are balanced in the way we give to our relationships and receive from them; we build trustworthiness and have a chance for peace and security. But when a family member is guilty of using or abusing me, he or she has violated what I am entitled to receive, and he or she is indebted to me. I am owed because I didn't get what I deserved — not to mention the fact that I may have tried to make up for what he or she did not give me by giving more (like a child trying to take care of a mother because the mother is unnurturing and self-absorbed). I have been ripped off and I hold the note from the person who abused me. This puts me in a one-up position vis-à-vis the person who victimized me and is indebted to me. The person who victimized me is one-down. These one-up, one-down positions make the work of forgiveness extremely difficult.

If I am one-up, I might feel that I am in a position of judgement since someone deserves to be judged for doing me wrong. Although I can use my judgement to assess the responsibility of my victimizer, if not careful, I may end up using my one-up position to feel superior; that is, I consider myself a better human being than my abuser and would never do such a thing as was done to me. When I take this superior, "holier than thou" position, my victimizer may feel justified in accusing me of being unreasonable and uncaring. He or she may by cut off, feeling that nothing can be done to move back into my good graces because of my unreasonable or uncaring expectations. This superior/ subordinate position of victim and victimizer makes understanding very difficult indeed.

What we have in common as victim and victimizer is our humanity. We are all born with natural gifts and abilities, and all of us are shaped by the experiences and actions of life. There were almost always mitigating circumstances in our past that helped to shed light on the actions we take or the attitudes we have, even when those actions result in our abusing innocent people or when those attitudes seem unjustified. As a victimizer, if I do not feel that I receive a fair hearing regarding the circumstances surrounding my unjustified or damaging actions; or more important, have not had an opportunity to express the injustice that I have experienced, then I will be defensive and therefore unresponsive to the demands of my victim. Every accusation that is thrown up by my victim will be answered or thwarted by an attack, excuse, or misdirection by me, the victimizer. But if my victim approaches me from a position of sameness or identification, I can hear much more clearly the complaint against me. As a victim, if I identify with my victimizer's past experiences, I realize that I am not superior to him or her. I might have made the same mistakes if I had been placed in his or her position.

Identification is the essential element in the second station of understanding. If I understand my abuser in terms of his or her position, limitations, development, efforts, and intent, I achieve an identification with that person. This identification is essential in that it acknowledges the fallibility of every human being, including myself. When I understand the person who has unjustly used or manipulated me, *I acknowledge that if I were placed in the same situation as my abuser, with his or her position, limitations, and development, I might make the same mistakes.* This is the crux of making identifications and doing the work of understanding in forgiveness. Identification stabilizes our positions as victim and victimizer and puts us on a level playing field where we are both fallible humans. When understanding and identification are achieved, a victim of unjustified violation or extreme abuse no longer feels one-up and will find it difficult to harbor blame or rage toward the victimizer. Victimizers, when understood and identified with, find it difficult to feel one-down and are likely to be less defensive and more receptive. Again, responsibility for the violation is not removed in understanding, but simply the blaming and condemnation that are painful reminders of abuse and carry little or no possibility for escape through resolution.

Step One: Discovering the Story of Your Violator

I am a backyard astronomer and love to search the sky for planets, comets, and galaxies. Every now and again, we are treated to a supernova, a giant explosion of a star that is giving its last show after using up all its nuclear fuel. Sometimes these are bright, and sometimes they are faint because of the great distance between the star and the earth. But one of the real "turn-ons" for me when I view a supernova or any great distant object is the thought that these phenomena actually took place hundreds, or even thousands, of years ago and it has taken that long for the light to reach the earth. What I see in the here and now is actually the past. It is a strange experience, how time and space turn on each other.

This is similar to how I experience families in my therapy office. I hear stories of how a family member has been particularly destructive, manipulative, or abusive. But most of the time, when this type of physical abuse, sexual assault, or neglect occurs, it is actually a present manifestation of actions and interactions that happened long ago. The truth is that almost all victimizers are victims themselves, usually through some type of dramatic damage in the past. This past abuse has now set the stage for the person to perpetuate the injustice and create their own legacy of abuse. If I were to look at the damage from a "here and now" perspective, it would be difficult for me to see anything but a victim and a victimizer, and very likely I would define the victimizer as culpable. It is only when I consider the past experiences of the victimizer that I can understand the original source of the pain and distress that caused this real person to take abusive actions that continued the legacy of family injustices.

In order to achieve understanding, we have to be willing to look at the pain or injury done to the person who did the injustice to us. As I stated in Chapter 2, when a person experiences an injustice or injury that denies him or her what he or she deserves from a relationship, then he or she is likely to be motivated to seek the entitlement from other relationships, such as with spouses or children. Unable to get what he or she wants or needs from these relationships because the spouse or children are unable or unwilling to fulfill old entitlements, the person turns to destructive manipulation or threats to try to make these current innocent relationships compensate for the abusive relationships of the past. When he or she uses destructive means to get what he or she wants, another injustice has occurred and a new generation of victimizer has emerged. The funny but sad truth about this dynamic is that the victimizer actually feels justified in carrying out the destructive action. People who damage others do not usually do so randomly; they do it because they feel violated, cheated, and damaged. Victimizers feel justified, or that they *deserve* to take destructive action to get what they need, even while they may hate its effects on others. They know that they are causing hurt, but since they have been cheated and abused in past relation-ships, they are entitled to use whatever means necessary to ensure that they are repaid for suffering violations. This can be seen in the story of an older man who was being confronted about physi-cally abusing his children when they were younger.

> "I know it was a terrible thing that you all experienced, but you tend to forget the good things that I did for you. I grew up in a family where I not only was beaten, but was sent out to earn my family's keep. I had to provide every-thing for them, just like I had to provide everything for you. I lost my temper, I know, and would do things to you that were wrong. But you should give me room for that mistake because I've always been under so much pressure to provide for everyone and keep the family afloat."

This father not only was physically abused as a child, but also was made to take a parental responsibility. He probably does feel that it was terrible to beat his children, but he also clearly feels like his children should excuse his behavior because he has ful-filled obligations in his family of origin that should not have been required of him. His children have suffered great harm at his hands, but he feels justified in asking that they excuse him because he was abused and misused as a child. However, these children have been denied their own just entitlement to love and trust. They do not feel that it is their job to make their father feel bet-ter because of his past abuse. They also feel ripped off and unjust-ly treated, and this will open them up to the same possibilities of seeking retribution or satisfaction in other relationships. Who will satisfy their need for justice? Most likely, they will seek the satis-faction from their own friends, spouses, or children, and these victims can become victimizers. One of my professors and col-leagues, Glen Jennings, summed up this concept: "It's like having the right script with the wrong actors." It is like playing out the script of *Romeo and Juliet* with the actors from *Othello*. The vic-tims of past injustices rightly feel pain and turmoil; they are, however, trying to get satisfaction from the wrong people.

This understanding of how our victimizers began as victims themselves is necessary if we are ever to really hear their stories. We must search out our victimizer's story, either by talking to the person directly or by gathering the information from other sources, such as friends or family. When we do so, identification with the wrongdoer is easier. Please note again, this identification with the wrongdoer does not suddenly make what he or she did to us right or trustworthy, or excuse him or her from responsibility for the wrong, but it does give us the boost we need to understand why someone whom we counted on would violate or abuse us. It helps us to answer the question of why without having to make our violator into a monster or make ourselves into worms.

I experienced this deeply in my own family. One of the things about my mother that used to really get under my skin was her saying that she was a good mother. I would think to myself, "You were a terrible mother! You abused us! You were out of control!" But years later when I started seeking out her story, I found a legacy of physical abuse had been passed along to her. Her father's idea of "discipline" was to tie his children to a fence, beat them with wire, and leave them there in the hot sun. He was said to have tied one of her brothers to a metal cattle pen in the back of a pickup truck and then driven over rocky roads to "beat the boy up a bit." When I started hearing these stories of my mother's past abuse, I began to think, "She's right. Compared with her father, she was a good parent." This did not excuse my mother's abuse of us, but it did help me identify with how she came to abuse her own children.

Step Two: Coming to Grips with Our Own Abusive Tendencies

It is painful to come from an abusive family. Even years later, I still deal with questions about my own adequacy as a human and whether or not I can trust people. But even more painful than coming from an abusive family is the fact that I myself have the tendency to be abusive.

Before I started working on forgiving my parents, I came up

with my own self-justifying solution for my abusive past. I swore emphatically that I would not have children. This was not a thoughtful choice, but a destructive and selfish tendency to make sure that I would always have all of my wife's affections and to hurt my parents by denying them the possibility of having any grandchildren. I was sure, at the time, that I was justified in my actions because of my history of abuse and that a superior person like myself would never do such terrible things as were done to me.

But try as I might to keep my self-righteous superiority, my abusive tendencies would always creep out from behind the strong wall that I constructed to hide them. When I first married, I would take great joy in tickling or "goosing" my wife in such a way that would hurt her. She hated it. I would do it and she would get angry and tell me to stop. I eventually would do it again. At one point, she looked at me with angry tears in her eyes and demanded that I stop. I finally did stop, but I can honestly tell you that I wanted to keep on with the mean pestering. It is strange, but my feeling was "If I want to tickle you, I will do it and you can't do anything about it. I'll do as I please." Here was the woman I loved asking me to stop doing something that caused her pain. I wanted to stop and yet I wanted to hurt her. I had always thought myself above abuse because I didn't consider myself capable of hitting my wife, but here was a clear desire to continue doing something that caused her pain. I felt I had a "right" to do as I pleased because I had been a victim of someone who had caused me pain. Even now, after years of working on my past abuse issues, I find myself feeling entitled to yell at, manhandle, or otherwise dominate my children when I get angry. I still have that feeling of destructive entitlement that tells me, "You were once victimized and it was wrong, so you shouldn't have to put up with others not doing what they should or what doesn't make you comfortable." It is an emotionally withholding position that makes those around me feel unloved and insecure. The truth is, it is abusive behavior.

It would be easy for me to say that I am superior to my parents. I would never abuse someone the way that I was abused as a child. However, when I look at my own abusive tendencies honestly, I come to a different conclusion. I am not as strong and psychologically "with it" as I think I am. I am fragile and weak. I am fearful and have been guilty of looking out for my own interests far more often than those of my family. When I consider these facts, I quickly realize that if I had grown up in my father's family with its instability and insecurity, or with my mother's family with a father who beat the children with wire, I might not do any better than they did as parents. This fact is enormously painful for me to face, but it is true.

We often think of ourselves as standing alone, as disconnected from the actions of our ancestors. I remember moving to Mississippi to take a position at the university. I believed I was opening up a new chapter in my family's history until I received a phone call from my mother informing me that her "people" were buried there. Sure enough, on her next visit, we went to a little church graveyard where there were rows and rows of headstones that bore my mother's maiden name. When we stood in front of my great-great-grandfather's Confederate headstone, I thought to myself, "I probably act and think more like this man than like any of my friends, and yet I know nothing about him." My mother's legacy of abuse, my legacy of abuse, came in part from him. We were, however, unaware of the details of his life and, therefore, of his influence on us. By and large, current transactions in any family or relationship are a result of influences from the past. Even in the best of situations, family members often say or do things to each other, and then are surprised, or even shocked, when they realize their destructive potential. When we have experienced extreme pain or violations from relationships, almost always the pain is eventually reflected in our own actions. When we recognize our own problems and abusive tendencies, then we realize that we, too, are capable of doing the same wrong to others that was done to us by our abusers.

Understanding and identification with the person who caused us pain can help us make sense of seemingly unrelated actions. For instance, when I confronted my mother about her threat to cut my wrists when I was eight years old, she gave me the following explanation:

"I'm not sure I remember the situation. I am sure, though, that what I was trying to do was scare you so that you would never do that again. I could not imagine why you would do such a thing, so I wanted to make sure that you wouldn't try it again."

Certainly this was the wrong decision. However, understanding that my mother came from an abusive place where fear and intimidation were used to motivate and change others makes it very easy for me to understand that her threat was prompted by an effort to change my behavior. Her choice was wrong, but it was motivated by a desire to keep me alive and not by a wish to get rid of me.

A final benefit of recognizing our own fallibility and abusive tendencies is that it gives us an additional boost of insight in stopping the transactions that assault others. When we rightly identify ourselves with the potential, and perhaps the history, of manipulating and threatening others in an unjustified way, then we are able to face more of the truth and change the way we behave. This is seen in the story of a young woman who struggled with depression and suicidal thoughts.

"My father was an alcoholic who sexually abused me. I felt as though he never loved me and was never there for me in an appropriate way. I always felt that he took an unfair advantage of me. My oldest daughter confronted me last week, telling me that when I withdraw and threaten to kill myself, it makes her feel like I'm not there for her. While other kids have a life, she says that she feels responsible for taking care of me. What I'm doing makes my daughter feel the same way that I felt growing up. I'm finding out that I'm not a whole lot different from my father. But I am going to make it different, I'm going to get some help."

Step Three: Releasing the Blame

Understanding helps in two directions. First, it helps us make person-to-person identification with our abusers or violators. Instead of being unreasonable beings who are programmed to cause damage, they become people, like us, who were placed in situations and roles that they did not handle well and in which they made unfortunate and tragic choices. The first two steps above assist in accomplishing this type of identification. Second, understanding helps us recognize the mitigating circumstances that lead to abuse. If I see how these circumstances shaped me, then I can believe that the same type of circumstances shaped the person who unjustly hurt me. The reason my abuser did not love me or is not trustworthy does not have to be that he, or she, or I was a terrible person. I realize that there were situations, circumstances, roles, and limitations that caused the unjust violation.

It is amazing to see just how many people who have unjustly suffered at the hands of another will blame themselves for the abuse or feel that they deserved the violation. This, of course, is a result of a person dealing with the pain of why he or she was not loved or treated in a trustworthy way by internalizing the shame of the abuse to mean that he or she is unlovable or undeserving. Also, an abused person often will remain loyal to the person who did the wrong because, since the victim himself or herself is unlovable or undeserving, he or she had better hold on to the relationship. This was the case for an abused woman who continued to allow her abusive husband to come home.

> "I am to blame. I mean, I know he shouldn't hit me or the kids, but I'm always doing something that is aggravating. I don't keep a good house. I let the kids get too loud. He says that I just let things go until he can't stand it anymore. If I would do better, he wouldn't get out of control. What needs to happen is that I do better."

Instead of making the husband responsible for his abusive actions, the woman bears the load of shame and assumes that she is the guilty one. This makes the work of forgiveness impossible. First, it excuses the real guilt of the husband. He must be held responsible if there is ever to be any sense of restoration of love and trust in any of the woman's relationships. Second, and more important, it puts the woman in a position where she will let whatever abuse occurs in any relationship be her fault because she has shamed herself into believing that it is. People will find it discouraging and problematic to have any normal give-and-take relationship with this woman.

In order to pursue understanding and release blame for abuse we received, we must be careful to ensure that we do not blame ourselves. Understanding means that we do identify with our victimizer's situation and past, but it also means that we resolve to hold him or her responsible for his or her actions. Instead of internalizing the pain and guilt to beliefs about ourselves, we must use the understanding to be better able to externalize the damage and recognize that our victimizer did these things because of his or her problems. In short, we must be careful not to let ourselves become beset by guilt and feel that we deserve the abuse, but instead to see ourselves as victims of unfortunate actions.

Although we run the risk of blaming ourselves for our victimization, often we become consumed with rage against the perpetrators. Instead of simply holding our victimizers responsible, we want to blame them. Understanding also gives us the ability to release the victimizer from the overwhelming culpability and to better recognize the factors that led to the abuse. When I understand the circumstances of the person who abused me, I am able to acknowledge the stresses and psychological impacts of the past on him or her and how they may have contributed to that person's damaging me. Then, I can actively start the process of releasing the person from the heavy burden of blame for his or her acts. I can see him or her as trying, much in the same way that I try, but failing and making choices that messed up his or her life. Such was the case for a man who had been manipulated into caring for his mother emotionally when he was a boy.

"She told me the story of how, when she was a girl, she and her mother were deserted by her father. She and her mother would hold each other and tell each other that they were going to be okay. She said that those were some of the only times that she felt secure. When my old man left, she said that she had made up her mind that she was going to give me the same thing that her mother had given her. There's no doubt that she used me to make herself feel better, but I do believe now that she had at least some desire to make me feel better during those times she was desperately holding onto me."

When we understand, we can see the person who did us wrong as struggling and trying to make sense out of life. This makes it possible, and sometimes easy, to release that person from bearing our rage and the blame associated with the past. I do not know whether or not people are inherently good or bad. But I do know that people make choices that turn out to be good or bad. Understanding the facts surrounding abusive or brutal actions contributes to a more balanced picture of the efforts and intentions that led to the choices made by the person who victimized another.

UNDERSTANDING AND THE WORK OF FORGIVENESS

When I go to a play or ballet, I seldom think about the people working behind the scenes. They exert a tremendous amount of effort beforehand, are constantly busy while the stage lights are on, and are left with the job of cleaning up afterward. Their contributions are necessary if the production is to succeed, but almost all of what they do is unseen by the audience. Understanding and the work of forgiveness can be compared to the work of the people who move the props and provide the sound for those on stage. It is mostly internalized work. We do not have to be in a relationship with the person who hurt us to do the work of understanding, nor do we ever have to communicate with that person again. But most people find that the work has enormous benefit in its ability to alleviate the pain engendered by rage and shame, and often results in our being able to see our victimizers in a different light, and even to relate to them in mutually beneficial ways.

Understanding allows us to confront the questions of why we

were not loved or treated in a trustworthy manner realistically, without having to rely on anger, rage, guilt, or shame to manipulate relationships. We are able to connect with the humanness of the perpetrators, and to see them as real people who made mistakes much in the same way that we make mistakes. But understanding also allows us to assess responsibility accurately. We can see the mistakes made by our victimizers and not be tempted to hold them overly culpable, or to make ourselves feel guilty for their wrongs. Most often, they are people who did bad things while trying to do the best they could. They are, however, still responsible. Understanding does not change the wrong. It just gives me the possibility of changing the pain that resulted from the wrong.

Special Focus Five:
Gaining Understanding

1. What are some of the circumstances and situations that shaped the person who caused you harm? (Talk to family and friends if you cannot talk to the person.)

2. What roles did the person who victimized you take on in the family in which he or she grew up?

3. How do you think these roles and circumstances may have influenced the person's unjustified action toward you?

4. If you had been in your victimizer's situation and with his or her limitations, what would you have done or how might you have responded?

5. Maintain the victimizer's guilt. Wrong actions are wrong actions, and you must maintain his or her responsibility. However, are there some circumstances that make you realize that he or she is not evil and that you are not unworthy or unlovable? If so, think about those things.

5

Station Three:

Giving the Opportunity for Compensation and Trust Building

You remember it as a child. You stepped up to the high diving board and stood in line for your first time going into the water from that height. As you climbed the ladder and watched person after person go over the edge and splash into the water, you thought, "It sure is getting high." And then you finally reached the top, and it was just you and the pool far below. Your thoughts raced along with your heart: "Should I go?" Fear and the desire for accomplishment collided in your head.

Maybe you jumped, maybe you didn't jump. But in either case you knew that once you took the leap off the diving board, you were committed to going all the way. Once you are over the edge, gravity has a way of insisting that you have no choice about going up. Many of our relationships in life present us with similar commitments. Whether the relationship is founded on marriage, friendship, finances, parenthood, or career, once we decide to leap, we are committed. Each new relationship brings with it the thrill of adventure and the possibility for growth, along with the fear of failure and hurt. But once the decision is made to engage in a new venture and relationship, we are changed by both the growth and the pain. In short, relationships are risky. Once we go over the edge, we are affected in ways that can be positive or negative. The real problem is that we do not know whether the effect will be good or bad until we actually step over the edge. Such is the nature of relationships, and of most of life.

The next station in the work of forgiveness, giving the opportunity for compensation, demands this type of risky commitment. The primary difference is that when we go about the work of forgiveness, we are stepping over the edge into a relationship that *we know* has injured us unjustly and did not have a positive effect. Often the relationship that caused us pain still has the potential to pay off and inspire growth and healing. To find out, however, we must step back into the relationship that hurt us before.

THE VALUE OF
RESTORATION VERSUS SALVAGE

For some of us who have been damaged in relationships in which we were abused, violated, or deserted, salvage achieved through the work of insight and understanding is the best we can do. We can be empowered by insight to see the root of our pain, prevent future interactions that will hurt us, and relieve ourselves of the burden of transferring our pain to other relationships. Understanding enables us to identify with the situation of the person who victimized us so that we can calm our inner turmoil of rage and shame. In the work of salvage, we can do better and feel better, and that makes us more understanding of ourselves and of current relationships. But salvage does not demand that we re-engage the prior relationship. In many cases, we may have been hurt by people with whom we never had a relationship. If I am raped by a stranger, do I have an obligation to restore our relationship? Certainly not. I had no relationship with the person in the first place. However, I can do the work of forgiveness through salvage. If I am abused by a spouse who denies any responsibility and refuses to change, am I obligated to restore the relationship? The answer is "No." Restoration is about restoring love and trust to the relationship. How can I maintain a relationship with someone who will hurt me in the same way again? To go back into a relationship and work for restoration when there is a clear intent to repeat the harm is not to be forgiving; it is foolish. Here, it is more appropriate to do the work of forgiveness through salvage. Salvage through insight and understanding is about dealing with the past in such a way that our burden of injustices need not be carried on into the future, but it does not put us back into a harmful relationship. There are many examples where limiting the work of forgiveness to salvage is not only wise, but is the only reasonable act of forgiving that can be accomplished.

But there will be other relationships that have caused us the same level of hurt — incest, rape, beatings, character annihilation — where we can see some possibility that things could be different. Perhaps it is just that the victimizer is now older and wiser. Maybe the person has changed his or her lifestyle in a way that makes us wonder about possible changes in our relationship with them. Perhaps I am in a situation in which I feel that I have to relate to the person in some way. These are the relationships that are amenable to restoration. But why would we want to reenter a relationship with anyone who once violated us by his or her actions?

The reason that restoration in the work of forgiveness is preferable where possible is that the very relationships that hurt us are those that hold the possibility of healing us. As we have mentioned before, the root of pain is the violation of fairness in a relationship or a person's not loving us or not being trustworthy. It is only within the context of relationships that I learn that I am lovable and that I can be secure in giving to others. When this is refuted by the way that someone violates me, then I have been cheated concerning what is rightfully mine. When the relationship is skewed by violation, I still have the opportunity to be taught by the person who damaged me that he or she was wrong, that I am indeed a lovable person and that I can be secure in relationships and trust that they will give me what I need. But I can only open up this new possibility of letting my violator rewrite my past programming by reopening myself to the relationship.

When it is possible to restore a relationship, it helps me keep all of my relationships clearer. I always exist in relationships in three contexts. First, I relate to the generations of people who made me or my parents and grandparents. I relate to these as a child, very dependent on the unconditional love and trustworthy giving they provide to me. Second, I relate to my equals, such as my siblings, my friends, and my spouse. I relate to these relationships as an adult exchange of giving to them in a fair exchange for what they give to me. Finally, I relate to the generations of people that will follow, whether through procreation or by my generativity. I relate to these as a parent, giving love and trustworthiness unconditionally so as to shape their views of themselves and their ideas about security in relationships. I exist in these three contexts simultaneously, so I am always relating as a child, as an adult, and as a parent. We have already discussed that when I am damaged in a relationship, but especially in a family relationship that I relate to as a child, I feel love and trust drained from me. I feel entitled to seek and get this love and trust where I can, which usually leads to threatening or manipulating the people from the other two contexts. When I work to restore the relationship that violated me, it clarifies which relationship owes me what. I am less tempted to go to innocent relationships because I am actively working on the elements of the violation with those who perpetuated it. The work of restoration almost always clarifies relationships for the victim.

Salvage through insight and understanding can ease my pain and have remarkable effects in helping me to be responsible and giving with others, but the original injustice of the abuse or violation always nags at me. I can stop myself from hurting others, but much of the work is self-gauging. I can never relax totally and go on automatic pilot. I am always keeping an eye on myself to make sure that my reactions and actions are appropriate to the relationship at hand and do not cause damage. To live in this way is certainly preferable to indulging in destructive behavior, but most of us would like to be in a position where our internal software, our original programming about love and trust, can be rewritten so that we could click into automatic pilot and not have to worry about causing others pain. This is what restoration in the work of forgiveness is about; providing the opportunity to repair the violations of love and trust.

How is it possible to repair damage that may have taken place many years ago? One of the great things about human beings is that they do not emerge as brand-new persons every year, but are accumulations of all that they were and are in their past and present. I am a grown man with children of my own, but I still carry with me the feelings and many of the perceptions of that eight-year-old boy who came to the conclusion that his family did not love him and would be better off without him. My eight-year-old self is still in there and available to me. My parents and I cannot go back to the past and do things differently, but who my parents were and who I was are still a part of *us*. The people they were who abused me and the boy who was abused are still present in some way. We are limited in that we cannot go back physically and undo the abuse, but we can go back emotionally and make it count in terms of love and trust.

I remember when I was a boy and my favorite dog was run over by a car. This was extremely painful for me because I was an insecure loner and that dog was about all I had. My mother and father dealt with me in a nonconfrontational way, but they were far from nurturing and supporting. I was left alone to do my work of grief and never brought it up in their presence.

A few years ago, my family and my wife's family suffered through the aftermath of a terrible crime. My wife's brother had been murdered with his date while he was attending college at the University of Oklahoma in 1970. Twenty years after the fact, charges were brought against a police officer for killing the two. I am not sure what the motivation was. Some people say they are sure that this former police officer was the murderer and that he was tried in an attempt to achieve justice. Others maintain that the district attorney just needed to try a high-profile case to move his career along. Whatever the case, I had to watch my family be tormented by the endless gory details of my brother-in-law's death while the prosecution had little hard proof. When a not-guilty verdict came in, our grief was overwhelming, not only because we remembered a brother and a friend, but also because we felt victimized by the justice system.

On the morning after the trial ended as I prepared to go to work, my mother showed up at my house to care for my children. She walked over and hugged me long and hard. She said, "I know this has been a terrible thing, but we are all going to get through it together. We will move on and stick together." The very first thing that popped into my head was the remembrance of my dog, something I had not thought about in some 30 years. I was sad, but I did not feel alone in my grief. That boy who had lost his dog and was frightened and sad was, and still is, in me. My mother's actions, years later, spoke to that boy and I was able to rewrite the crucial story about grieving.

This is the magical part of relationships and restoration. Relationships carry the power to heal old wounds. Restoration means that we return to the relational issues as they were when they caused us damage. When we arrive on the emotional scene where the love and trust were violated, we open ourselves up to those relationships and the possibility that whoever hurt us unjustly is now, at least in part, able to give us the love and trust we deserve. When we take this risk and our past victimizer loves us and gives to us in a trustworthy way, we really experience a rebirth of the relationship. Restoration provides a way for the entitlement of love and trust in a relationship to be satisfied, even if that love and trust never existed. In this way, restoration in the work of forgiveness is a unique human possibility that has the possibility not only of *easing* our pain, but of *healing* it as well.

There are two stations in the work of restoration. *Giving the opportunity for compensation* means that we provide our victimizer with the opportunity to "prove" himself or herself as loving and trustworthy by allowing interactions that permit varying degrees of vulnerability on both of our parts. With this station, the original injustice or violation may never be directly discussed. In *overt forgiving*, the victim and victimizer bring up the violation or abuse directly in order to talk about the wrong, assign responsibility, and move the relationship to a restored status that will not be hindered by the past. Both stations are equally valid ways to restore a relationship and are appropriate in different situations. Both require risk, commitment, time, and work for both the victim and victimizer.

But be aware of the ramifications. Restoration demands that we re-enter a relationship with the very people who hurt us unjustly. You must not take this risk lightly. If you take the risk, it will mean that you are vulnerable and your victimizer may choose to abuse, use, or manipulate you again. I often hear uninformed people, in talking about forgiveness, say that if you do not forgive, you are only hurting yourself. A thread of this may be true — if we harbor rage and shame, we do ourselves harm — but the fact is that if I try to restore a relationship with someone who has hurt me once, I may be hurt twice. There is no guarantee that if I try to restore a relationship, I will not be hurt again. I have something very real to lose. I may be violated again, which will make my pain worse. I must consider carefully whether salvage or restoration is appropriate to my situation.

ARE YOU READY FOR RESTORATION?

The work of forgiveness is actually sloppy and undefined. It happens at different rates and in different ways for different people. Some do the work in only one of the four stations, and that is it for the rest of their lives. Some do a little here, then stop, and then continue the work later in a different station. For some, forgiveness is sudden and dramatic during a face-to-face confrontation. For others, it proceeds a little at a time over a long period. A few people will do the work of forgiveness outlined in this book in sequence. They will do some insight, then understanding, then proceed to giving the opportunity for compensation, and eventually confront their violators and achieve overt forgiving. But that is not how it happens for most people. The stations are not stages. Most of us will do the work of forgiveness by oscillating among the stations of insight, understanding, giving the opportunity for compensation, and overt forgiving many times and to different degrees. So when I discuss readiness for restoration, I do not mean that these suggestions are requirements to be met before you proceed. They are simply meant to give you some indication as to whether or not it is a good idea to try to restore a relationship. However, you are the final judge of what is right for you. Many people have achieved restoration by knowing that it was the right time for them and their violators even though the indications did not seem to promise success.

Salvage

There is little doubt in my mind but that the work of salvage in insight and understanding goes a long way toward preparing you for the work of restoration. When you know what the violation is, you clearly see how it was perpetuated, and you realize how to stop yourself from making the same mistakes, since you are wise to the interactions and problems in the relationship. This helps you to set effective boundaries and to be in a formerly abusive or manipulative relationship with less risk. You can give your victimizer a detailed description, if needed, of the specifics of the violation and injustice. Through the work of understanding, you can better identify with the victimizer and will be less driven by emotions that are based on shame or rage.

Acceptance

Many people go into the work of forgiveness through restoration with the idea that the violator will be able to obliterate the memory of the abuse or manipulation. They think that if the abuser acts differently in the here and now, that will mean that the past never really happened. However, when we have been damaged by an injustice, we need to accept the fact that the scars cannot simply be erased. We cannot engage in a game where we constantly ask how we would be different if we could remove the past damage. Past violation is a reality. It is part of who we are in the way it has shaped and motivated us. While it is natural to grieve this damage, we cannot make it different. It is like the man or woman who loses his or her spouse to death after a happy marriage. He or she may long to have the partner back, but not dealing with the reality of death will trap the person in a grief that will prevent him or her from ever functioning healthily again. If we get stuck in the mourning over damage and only long for its removal, we will get bogged down in our effort to restore our emotional health.

Acceptance means that we see ourselves as innocent victims of another's unjust behavior and reckon with the damage that it has caused. We hold our victimizer accountable for his or her actions and expect that he or she will behave differently in the future as a testimony to the desire to make up for the past violation.

Willingness

At some point during the work of forgiveness in restoration, a victim has to be willing to let the victimizer take responsibility for his or her actions. When someone beats me up or steals from me, I pursue the person doggedly, demanding that he or she be held responsible and be punished. I hold onto the past because I was violated and must see to it that my perpetrator is held responsible. But when I enter the work of restoration, I am in essence saying that my victimizer will now take responsibility for his or her past actions and pay for the past irresponsibility with his or her loving and trustworthy actions. I am saying that I am willing to release the victimizer from the need for punishment and allow him or her to make things right with me. Too often, people will pursue a relationship with their victimizer, only to accuse the wrongdoer over and over again. Willingness means that we are reasonably sure we can pursue a continuing relationship with our violator without the need to punish him or her or hold past offenses over his or her head, and accept his or her efforts to restore the status of love and trust.

Realism

When we try to restore a relationship with someone who has done us wrong, it is reasonable to expect the violator to make an effort to do loving and trustworthy things. However, it is unreasonable to expect that our victimizers of the past will never do anything that is unloving or untrustworthy. People are imperfect. Just because a violator or wrongdoer says that he or she has repented and wants to do good, that does not mean that good will always be done. When we work in restoration, we need to be realistic in our expectations of ourselves and our victimizers. There will be situations where we say we forgive, only to confront a memory or situation that triggers an anger, shame, or depression that we take out on the one we forgave. Those who hurt us in the past and with whom we are working to restore love and trust will make mistakes, both intentionally and unintentionally, that will cause us to question whether the effort is worth it or if the restoration process is true progress. We must be realistic. Given our own and our victimizer's fallibility, there will be times when we muddle along and progress is difficult. Realism means that we recognize that restoration is a "two steps forward, one step back" process.

Commitment

Restoration is risky and, therefore, scary. Think about it. Here is a person who is responsible for a horrendous crime against our being. Just being around the person is alarming and threatening. If you are going to be able to live with that kind of threat and fear, then you must be convinced of the value of pursuing restoration. If you doubt the value of the relationship in healing you, then you will likely lack the commitment necessary to make the healing of the relationship possible. Only when you feel that restoring the relationship between you and your victimizer is necessary to your well-being, and are convinced of the value of such a restoration to your future relationships, will you have the commitment necessary to deal with the fear and risk that reconnecting with a past abuser demands. You must be a true believer to restore a relationship. If you are not, you will always be trying to escape when the going gets tough. We either step off the diving board into the relationship, or we do not.

Unfortunately, we can never know for sure whether a past destructive relationship will be healing or will continue to be destructive. The best we can do is to evaluate the relationship in terms of its potential for healing. I must judge whether or not I am willing to stay in such a threatening situation with the person who hurt me. I must judge if the relationship is one that is necessary or important to me. Finally, I must judge whether the person who unjustly damaged me is now able to love me and treat me in a trustworthy manner. This is difficult to do, because we never really know the thoughts and emotions of another person.

Special Focus Six: Readiness for Restoration

1. Have you taken steps in your relationship with this person to ensure that you have enough power to protect yourself? What are these steps?

2. Are you able to identify with this person's past history that may have influenced him or her to violate you? If so, how do you think his or her past would have affected you if you had lived in his or her place?

3. If this relationship were restored to being trustworthy and loving, how would you know that things were better? (Watch out for such statements as "I would forget the past.")

4. Are there circumstances where you can imagine this person changing enough for you to have a normal relationship with him or her?

5. How many trials is this person allowed if you try to rebuild a relationship with him or her? (Be cautious if you are demanding perfection from him or her.)

6. If this relationship were restored, would you be better off than you currently are? (That is, emotionally, socially, and physically.)

GIVING THE OPPORTUNITY FOR COMPENSATION

Imagine that I asked you to give me your hand and you reached out to me. While you were reaching, I pulled out a knife and slashed your hand. Then I told you that I would bandage the cut, and to just give me your hand. Would you do it again? Of course not! You would only let me touch your wound if you had reason to believe that I did have the first-aid equipment and my intentions had changed radically.

Giving the opportunity for compensation is much like this. The person who caused us the injury is now the one that we are looking to for treatment of our damaged emotions and self. At this station in the work of forgiveness, we may be a little unsure of how trustworthy and loving our victimizer may be. In order to address this problem without just sticking a hand out and perhaps getting slashed again, we ask for evidence that the victimizer is now trustworthy. Trustworthiness and love are restored by allowing our victimizers to rebuild their status in the relationship in a progressive manner. As the victimizer proves that he or she is loving and trustworthy now, the remembrances of the past violations begin to fade. The original violation or abuse may never be discussed directly. No apology or promise may ever be exchanged. In giving the opportunity for compensation, the victim gives the victimizer a chance to pile one trustworthy and loving act on another until, finally, the relationship can be declared loving and trustworthy.

It works like this. Say I declared bankruptcy and defaulted on many of my loans and bills. If I then went to my bank and requested a loan of $25,000 to buy a new car, I would be thrown out on my ear! My banker would angrily tell me, "You cheated us and ripped us off once, and you won't do it again." He would be right to feel this way. But if, after declaring bankruptcy, I went to my banker and said, "I know that I have been financially irresponsible in the past, but I also know I need a line of credit. What I would ask is that you lend me $100 and I will pay it back at the rate of $50 a week for two weeks." My banker is much more likely to take the $100 risk. If he lends me the money and I pay it back in two installments, I might go back and say, "Now I would like to borrow $200 and pay it back at $25 a week over the next two months." If I am true to my word, then I could probably get a $400 loan to pay back over two or three months. If I kept borrowing ever-increasing amounts of money and paying them back faithfully, then after 12 to 18 months, I would probably be granted a loan of $5,000 to buy a used car. It is not that I have always been financially stable, but the memory of my past irresponsibility has now faded in the light of my current trustworthiness.

Giving the opportunity for compensation works in the same way. As the person who victimized me demonstrates that he or she is now able to be responsible in giving and receiving in a balanced and fair relationship, the more vulnerable and trusting I can become. The more vulnerable I become, the deeper the level at which interactions can take place and the more trusting and loving our relationship can become. It simply means giving the wrongdoer the chance to prove that he or she will not do it again and that he or she is capable of love and worthy of trust. This process of rebuilding love and trustworthiness is usually established a little at a time over a long period. As love and trust in the relationship are demonstrated, they tend to generate more love and trust between us and our victimizer. This increase of resources not only helps in healing our past wounds, but builds strength to address the relational challenges of the future.

Many of the people with whom I work in therapy like this station of forgiveness because it provides the opportunity for relationship restoration while minimizing their risk of being hurt again. This station does not demand that the damage be discussed with our violator, which means that both of us can approach the other without having to be defensive about the past. It gets us around the potential for accusation and counter-accusation. This station is also good in that it takes into account the fact that our victimizer may have changed since he or she hurt us. By giving the victimizer small opportunities to demonstrate change, we can gauge whether there has been a development of giving resources in our violator. Finally, giving the opportunity for compensation provides both us and our victimizers with multiple chances to address past wrongs. Most of the damage that happens to us is not caused by one action, but is accumulative. It is unreasonable for us or our violators to think that the work of forgiveness can be accomplished in one meeting. Most often, we need time to rebuild trustworthiness in relationships. We did not get into the mess in one day and we cannot expect to get out of it in one day. This station allows for the development of trust through multiple relational exchanges between us and our victimizer.

Step One: Conceptualizing a "Payment Plan"

Wrong is not perceived as a wrong. It is wrong. If you have been a victim of someone's abuse or manipulation, it is not so much based in your perception as it is in the violator's action. This is not to say that there are not some situations in which we honestly differ in our beliefs about family injury. But the kinds of injuries I talk about are the ones that involved physical or sexual acts or emotional burdens that should have been assumed by somebody else. In most of these situations to which I refer, even a five-year-old would know that there is a relational injustice. If you have suffered a violation, you are an innocent victim of an unjust crime against relational love and trust. You may have suffered emotionally, physically, socially, and spiritually. You have a *justified* claim against your perpetrator.

The restoration problem in using the station of giving the opportunity for compensation lies in this justified claim. Many times, the victimizer or perpetrator cannot make up for the pain and damage that he or she inflicted; not to the same degree. For instance, consider the story of a young girl who was scalded by her father.

> "My father would go crazy when I wouldn't do what he told me to do. He would keep the hot water heater up as high as it would go, then fill a tub with water and threaten to throw me in if I didn't mind. Well, one time he actually forced me into the tub, he was so mad. I blistered all over

the bottom half of my body. I still carry around scars because of him."

Even if this woman brings herself to wanting to restore the relationship with her father, how can he compensate her for the emotional and physical damage he caused? The truth is that he cannot. He can dedicate himself to living in a loving and trustworthy way, but he cannot make up entirely for the damage. For restoration to take place between this daughter and her father, the daughter would have to be willing to accept his efforts toward love and trust as payment for the wrong incurred. This is much like a bank's taking 20 cents on every dollar owed to them. When a wrong is done, the victimizer seldom can make the situation totally right. We are left, instead, with having to make decisions about how much compensation will be enough to call the situation right. It does not mean that we cancel out the indebtedness of our victimizer, but that we are willing to accept a payment plan. Sometimes these plans are explicit between us and our victimizers, but most often we create them in our own heads. Such was the case with a woman who was repeatedly abused sexually by her father while she was growing up.

> "I can see the ways that he has changed. He is much better to my mother and he keeps his distance from me. I will ask him to do things at my house when I am not there, like fix the sink or paint a closet. He has done it every time. I can imagine a time where I can sit in the same room with him. If he can keep his eyes to himself and on my mother, there might be a time that we can be in the same house together again."

The implication here is clear. If the father who sexually abused this woman continues to treat her in a giving way without expecting anything in return and, more important, acts appropriately with his own wife, then the daughter can accept his actions as payment against the wrong he has done to her. She eventually will be able to reach the point where she can be in his presence and trust that he will not act inappropriately. In this way, this daughter is willing to give up her claim of injustice on the part of the father and let him take steps to prove his good intentions. In this case, the claim was unspoken between the daughter and father. But there are cases where the claim is very explicit, such as this one in which another father sexually abused his daughter.

DAUGHTER: I feel that you have taken something away from me emotionally that cannot be made up.

FATHER: I know what you mean, I have trouble talking about it.

DAUGHTER: I do, too. But I have to know that this has cost you something if we are going to be able to put things back together.

FATHER: I would do anything if it would help you see that I have suffered and want things better.

DAUGHTER: You hurt me emotionally. I know that money is very important to you, so I want you to pay for some things to prove that you are sorry.

FATHER: Like what?

DAUGHTER: I want you to pay for my therapy. I want you to pay for my graduate education. I want you to pay for my wedding.

FATHER: (after thinking several minutes) You think this would help?

DAUGHTER: I know that you say you are sorry, but to do what I'm asking, I think you would have to take out loans and maybe even get another job. It would say to me that you are really serious about paying the price to get our relationship back. Yes, I think it would help.

FATHER: (after several minutes) I'll do it. I can see what you mean.

Here, the woman has very specific ideas about how she wants

the father to prove his changed behavior. She reasons that he cost her emotionally, so it would be fair for her to cost him financially. As the father carries out his financial commitment, the daughter will likely be able to see him as a changed man and trust him more.

In order to conceptualize how a victimizer can compensate us for our pain, we actually have to give to the victimizer. We give in the sense that we provide a way for the person who did the wrong to pursue a normal relationship. We must be willing to set aside the imbalance and allow for incremental trust opportunities and exchanges. But we must also be willing to admit that we will eventually have to fulfill our obligations to the relationship. If we see giving the opportunity for compensation as a license to demand that the wrongdoer make up for the violation for the rest of his or her life, then he or she eventually will realize that there is no payment plan. The victim who is never willing to fulfill obligations will feel perpetual hopelessness as he or she bears the burden of being owed a debt that cannot be repaid in full. Such was the case with a woman who, having had a extramarital affair, tried to rebuild trust between herself and her husband.

> "You can ask him. He will tell you that I have done all that he has asked. For three years, I have not been out of his sight or any place without his knowledge. I have apologized so many times. I have worked with his rules, even when it was not fair. I have done it because I really wanted things to be right; I wanted to make up for what I did. But he is just the same now as the first day I told him. He is stone cold. I know now that he just cannot ever give to me after what I did to him. He can't give to me and I just can't go on without getting anything from him."

In giving the opportunity for compensation, we not only have to give up our claim for full "payment" for the injustice that we experienced and conceptualize what "payment" our victimizer can make, but we must also prepare ourselves concerning what we have to do to move back into giving in the relationship. In this way, this station is really *fore-giving* on our part. We sacrifice what is owed us and commit ourselves to fulfilling our obligations in the relationship before the victimizer has fully proved his or her love or trustworthiness.

In conceptualizing a payment plan, I believe it is helpful to start off with victimizers in ways that put us at minimum risk and afford the opportunity for success. For instance, I ask most people who pursue this course to begin by dropping their abuser a card or short note. If they receive an appropriate response, I suggest a longer letter. If a promising response is returned, then a short phone call may be in order. If the conversation is trustworthy, eventually perhaps a short face-to-face visit can be arranged. Each interaction involves a little more risk for the victim, but if the victimizer has proved trustworthy at the previous steps, one might risk one's vulnerability.

Step Two: Sticking with the Plan, Making Allowances

Whenever I think about the work of forgiveness and restoration through giving the opportunity for compensation, I think about a good coach preparing a runner for a big race. Any coach knows that you want your athlete to peak on the day of the race. He or she knows that the runner will have good days and bad days, and that persisting through the bad days is an important aspect of conditioning. Also, a good coach realizes that you must stick to a training schedule to build strength and endurance and have the work culminate on the day of the race.

Giving the opportunity for compensation is similar to the idea of a "race day." It is important to have a plan, but you must be willing to stay with it in the same way that you would stick to a training schedule. The primary idea in this station is to rebuild the status of love and trust with actions that prove the violator to be loving and trustworthy, even after a severe violation. This usually does not happen all at once. It takes time for both the victim and the victimizer to develop a sense of new direction in the relationship. It is not unusual to not have communicated with a victimizer for a long time or to have had unpleasant interactions with him or her for most of our lives. It makes it important, therefore, to *pace* the interaction a bit so that you and the victimizer can establish some baseline of trustworthy behaviors and a good idea of how the relationship will progress. When you create too many interactions too quickly, you simply do not have the strong trust in your victimizer needed to develop more complex interactions. Such was the case with a woman who had been neglected emotionally by her mother for years. There had always been a distance between the two, but the mother was anxious to make up for the past injury.

> "I called Mom and we had a very good conversation. She expressed interest in my kids and said that she really did want to know me better. I responded by saying that maybe we could talk more often. Well, she has called every day. She wants to come and visit. There is nothing wrong with the conversations; she really is taking an interest in me that seems genuine without being manipulative. But it is just too much. My mother was absent from my life so long that I just am not sure I can trust her. When she calls too much, it makes me stand off because I am not ready to dive into that deep a relationship that quickly."

In this situation, the daughter does not have the foundation of trust necessary to support the degree of interaction the mother wants. It would be better for her to stick with the plan or only talk a few times at the daughter's pace rather than have the interactions become more and more strained because the daughter struggles to maintain her distance.

Staying with a slow and sequential plan is also good for the past victimizer because it tells him or her which boundaries to respect. When we give our past violators conflicting messages concerning the speed or consistency of reconciliation, it confuses them and leads to incorrect guessing as to what we want from them. Such was the case with this mother who had physically abused her daughter. The daughter had initiated the process of

giving the opportunity for compensation with her, but the relationship was strained.

> "I'm never really sure how to act. When she [the daughter]
> first called and said that she wanted to go slow and build
> back a relationship, I asked what 'go slow' meant. She said
> for us to talk twice over the next month to see how it
> went. The first time was fine, but the second time we
> talked, I could tell something was wrong. I finally got out
> of her that she was hurt that I had not written to her dur-
> ing that time or asked to stop by. I apologized and then
> started dropping by. Now she has told me that I am push-
> ing too fast. I'm not sure what I'm supposed to do. If I
> don't do enough, it is bad; if I do too much, it is bad."

Although it is understandable, the daughter is not sticking to
a plan that the mother can understand. At one time the daughter
wishes to keep a comfortable distance, and another time she wants
her mother to become more involved. It is always better for us
and our victimizers to look at the process of restoration through
giving the opportunity for compensation as long-haul training.
When we switch our expectations and plans midstream, it throws
off our schedule and leaves us and our victimizers confused.

As I mentioned before, a good coach knows that athletes are
going to have good days and bad days. As I work with people
who are in the process of giving the opportunity for compensation, I find that it is usually not the victimizer who has the problem of allowing for bad days but, most often, the victim. Our victimizers have damaged us tremendously and we are rightly wary
of re-entering a relationship with them at any level; but, as I
pointed out before, people are not perfect and our victimizers will
have bad days in which they will say or do manipulative things
that will make us feel abused all over again. In doing the work in
this station, not only is it necessary for us to adhere to our plan
of compensation, but we must also make allowances for our victimizers when they do not live up to our expectations. Only in

this way will we eventually make progress in the relationship. For instance, consider the struggle of a young woman who is seeking to reestablish a relationship with her neglectful, manipulative, and alcoholic mother.

> "I know that things have been progressing. She has been very careful in what she has been saying to me, no comments about why I haven't called or how lonely she has been. But at the end of the conversation yesterday, she said that sometimes she just wanted me to make her feel better. It made me realize that my mother has not changed a bit. She will always be wanting me to say things that make her feel better about how she has screwed up her own life. Those little things that she has been doing lately are just covering up the real her. I can never trust any change she makes."

The mother of this woman has probably spent 50 years as a manipulative alcoholic. Being given the opportunity to change means that she has to rework the old patterns, habits, and thought processes. She probably is just covering her manipulative self, but the fact that she is trying to do that is an expression of her desire to become loving and trustworthy. It would take a long time for her to totally eradicate the patterns and behaviors associated with alcoholism. The daughter's expectation that the mother would never again manipulate her is well intentioned, and maybe even justified, but it is not realistic. When we enter into giving the opportunity for compensation, our victimizers will hurt us again. However, we must expect to make allowances for these stumbles. If the damaging acts are too consistent, then they wipe out any potential of relational progress and we are probably best advised to do the work of forgiveness in salvage. But as for the occasional transgressions of the wrongdoers, we must hang in there with the plan and make allowances for their bad days.

Step Three: Making the Efforts of the Victimizer Count
One of the problems in restoration by giving the opportunity

for compensation is that it is usually a slow process with sequentially small steps toward improving the relationship. Yesterday, or even six months ago, may look much the same when you are making slow progress in a relationship. It is difficult, therefore, to know exactly when the relationship is "better" or has improved to the point where it is loving and trustworthy. To ensure that the loving and trustworthy efforts of our victimizers count in improving the relationship, we provide markers or make clear statements as to how the relationship has improved.

A marker of relational improvement can be anything from a ritual we perform to simply a statement made to our abuser. But the point of such markers is to make clear in our minds where the change in the relationship has taken place and to give our abusers encouragement that their efforts have mattered and are noticed. An example of using a ritual to mark relational improvement is the story of a woman who had been physically abused by her husband.

"We had been separated for six months and he really took it to heart to change. I asked him to go to therapy and work on his anger, and he did. He has been very giving to me and the children. It was time to get back together. Since all of our friends had stood beside us and helped us while we worked on things, I decided it would be nice to have a little reception at which we would announce that we were getting back together. It was sort of like a wedding reception. But we also told everyone, and each other, that we would continue to work on changing our relationship. It was really helpful to realize how much work we had done and the things that we have to do in the future."

The markers can also represent a realization reached by us and simply verbalized to our abuser. Such was the case with a woman who had been physically and emotionally abused by her mother when she was a child.

"I was home at Thanksgiving and my mother and I were doing the dishes after the meal. It just came to me, the realization that we had done a lot of work to make things better. It just felt at that moment like this is what daughters and mothers do. I looked at her and said that we had come a long way. She gave me a long stare, and then a good hug. It was like we were over a major hurdle."

Forgiveness and restoration are tough. In the midst of our fears and remembrances of the past, we have to actively acknowledge in our minds that things are better. This confronts our fears head-on and gives us important markers of relational progress to point to when we encounter hard or untrustworthy times. Letting our realizations of improvement wash through our lives helps us to heal and to make the efforts of our abusers count.

ALLOWING COMPENSATION AND THE WORK OF FORGIVENESS TO HAPPEN

Some would say that if forgiveness takes place over time, it really is not forgiveness at all. Some would say that to forgive, you have to release your claim for justice and let the violator go. If you keep going, saying that the violator must do something more, it is not forgiveness. Perhaps in a perfect world, this is true. I wish that I could be 100 percent forgiving of the wrongs done to me and never feel affected or trapped by my lack of trust in someone who damaged me. But I am not perfect. The truth is that I can only forgive 60 percent of the wrongs against me and I need some evidence or help to get me to 70 percent of forgiveness. It takes time. Does that lessen the impact of forgiveness and restoration? Maybe. But it is the only way that some of us can get to the point of crawling back into a relationship with someone who has done us harm. If the eventual end is restoration of love and trust after tremendous damage, then I think that it well qualifies for the work of forgiveness.

In many ways, this station of forgiveness is the most courageous to undertake because neither the victim nor the victimizer
knows exactly where the efforts will lead. Like two mountain
climbers, they commit to tying themselves together to attack the
formidable task of conquering their past violations without absolute
clarity as to how to do it. Sometimes the victim takes a few steps,
sometimes it is the victimizer. Both lead and follow at times. Both
watch each other carefully. Sometimes, one or both fall and must
get up to tackle the task again. But if both are intent on getting
up to the point where they are secure in love and trust, they will
struggle and eventually get there. I think that that takes remarkable courage and commitment and certainly looks like forgiving.

Special Focus Seven:
Getting Started In Giving the Opportunity
for Compensation

1. When you think about the violation, what are some possible
    ways this person could prove to you that he or she is trust-
    worthy or loving?

2. How much time would be fair for you to allow this person
    to show that he or she is trustworthy or loving?

3. Try to list 10 (yes, 10) steps or interactions that you could
    take with this person that would eventually lead to a restored
    relationship. Make sure that the beginning steps are small and
    ones that do not require much risk or expectation from
    either side.

4. Everybody fails. Out of these 10 steps or interactions, how
    many do you think it is fair to expect not to be totally suc-
    cessful in achieving?

5. If the person does everything on your list, how would you
    go about telling him or her that or recognizing the work that
    had taken place?

6

Station Four:

Overt Forgiving and
Restoring the Relationship

---

*U*s. Us is invisible, but is still a living being. I think about this concept often when I think about my relationship with my wife. I love my wife and she has made all the difference in my life. As much as I would miss her if she were gone, however, I think that I would miss what we are together more. I would miss *us*. Our *us* is different from just Sharon and Terry added together. It is born of our sacrifice and desire to form our relationship. Our *us* has a personality of its own. I can predict when *us* is getting ready to fight or what *us* will say next in a conversation. I do not particularly care for ballet, but our *us* does like ballet.

It is a wonderful thing in relationships when an *us* is formed. What is formed in the *us* is more than the compilation of our parts from individuals. It is an invisible bond that makes us one with another person, not because we obliterate our individuality, but because a whole new, different, and living *us* comes into being. It is a unique birth experience between humans who have an intimate relationship.

The food and water that keep the *us* alive in our relationships are love and trust. If I care for you, love you, and maintain an attitude and action that sacrifices part of what I want individually for your good, and you do the same, we create a strong and healthy relationship. Our *us* is viable and vibrant because we freely give to each other through the relationship, and we are taught and changed individually through the intimacy of us. If, however, I am violated, abused, or manipulated by my relational partner, I start withholding and protecting myself. I cannot give freely because I will be hurt and damaged through the relationship. I withdraw and become fearful of *us*. Our *us* becomes weaker as it is denied the essential life-giving elements of love and trust. Unfortunately, not only are there assaults and violent acts that damage and weaken *us*, but there are also acts of abuse and manipulation that kill *us* off and end the relationship. If I am a victim of abuse or violence, often it is a matter of survival. I may feel that the only way that I, as an individual, can survive is to withdraw from the relationship and put an end to *us*. It may make me sad and hurt me terribly, but it may come down to a choice between me and the relationship.

These are the situations in which forgiveness through restoration is so powerful. When relationships are damaging due to violence or manipulation, *us* has actually been put to death. We cannot open ourselves up to the possibility of our abusers hurting us, so we have to withdraw giving. This, in turn, closes off love and trust in the relationship and starves *us*. The work of forgiveness in the first three stations — insight, understanding, and giving the opportunity for compensation — is designed to help us come to grips with the reality of the relationship, to do better in current and future relationships, and perhaps to revive the relationship gradually and sequentially. In the fourth station of forgiveness, overt forgiving, the relational restoration is much more sudden and dramatic. In this station, two people come together after their *us* relationship has become very weak or has died, and work together to revive and re-birth the relationship at one sitting. In overt forgiving, we work with our abuser to restore and rebuild love and trust on the spot and a new relational *us* comes into life.

OVERT FORGIVING

Some points in time can be enormously life-changing. We mark some of these points that change our lives. When we graduate or marry, we know that things are now different in terms of our responsibilities and expectations. When we move out of our parents' home, we realize that we have embarked on a new phase of development. If you have children, you probably remember the change in perspective when you became a parent. Points in time can and do change us throughout our lives.

Overt forgiving is like this. At a point in time, this fourth station in the work of forgiveness focuses immense effort on and stresses the importance of the interactions between the innocent victim of a violation and the perpetrator of that violation. Often, overt forgiving represents the culmination of time and work in the other stations of forgiveness that resulted in enough love and trust to enable direct discussion of past damage. Sometimes, however, overt forgiving is the first step back into the relationship for victim and victimizer as they pledge to walk away from the meeting to live in loving and trustworthy ways. In cases where overt forgiving is the culmination of much work in the other stations, the meeting between victim and victimizer is like the first stroll over a newly constructed bridge. The two have been constructing a sound relational bridge through insight, understanding, and giving the opportunity for compensation. Overt forgiving is the act of sealing their agreement that they are now different in the way they relate and that the past has been resolved. In situations where overt forgiving is the first step back into the relationship, the victim and victimizer erect a temporary bridge over the past hurt and pain, and then ease out on it to start reinforcing the structure, to make it strong and stable over time. But in both situations, the victim and victimizer are directly confronting the past violations and pain at a point in time with the intention of facilitating compassion, courage, and the commitment to making the relationship different.

Giving the opportunity for compensation restores the relationship a little at a time over a long period as we relate to our victimizers in more complex and trustworthy ways. Overt forgiving is different in that we meet face to face with the victimizer and talk about the past offenses, with the intention of addressing them once and for all. Instead of a payment plan whereby the victimizer gradually demonstrates trustworthiness and love that eventually erases the debt of the violation, we essentially cancel out the victim's indebtedness and release our claim to the injustice. In discussing the violation and forgiveness openly, we come to a point where we agree to relate to each other in a new way that is unhindered by the violation of the past. Overt forgiving is a new covenant or contract in the balance of give-and-take between us and our victimizer.

Responsibility and Overt Forgiving

Your pain from relational abuse may be quite profound, even though the source of the pain may vary. Some of us will be victims of being used inappropriately by someone who took advantage of us, such as a divorced parent's making us emotionally responsible for his or her welfare. Some of us will be neglected and denied what we deserved because our relational partner was addicted to drugs or alcohol, to the point where the substance was more important to them than we were. Others of us were simply used to make our parents or close relationships look good, and we learned that what we did was more important than who we were. Still others of us were subjected to the violent acts of sexual or physical exploitation. We were denied the love and trust we deserved.

There are, however, different perspectives on this abuse, depending on whether you are an abused person or an abuser. I was physically abused by my parents, but they believe that they did a better job at parenting than had their parents. You see the same difference in perspective from a young woman who was reeling from pain and self-doubt related to her father's not giving her love and nurture.

"I remember as a child being so scared and alone. I had a stable home, everything was provided for me, but I always felt so incompetent. My father would never show any feeling at all for me. I remember one time, as a little girl, going to him with tears in my eyes and saying that all of my classmates were better than me. I asked him if I was okay, what he thought of me. He stared at me for a few seconds and then just walked away. I just knew then that I wasn't okay. If my own father couldn't tell me I was okay, then I wasn't."

Why would a father inflict such pain on his daughter? He was a good provider and maintained a stable environment for his family. Surely his failure to nurture his daughter emotionally came out of spite or meanness. We abhor the father's neglect until we hear his story.

"I've never been able to face this. My father was irresponsible and left my mother right after I was born. She was always depressed. I remember when I was four, we left for California without packing anything. She kept on saying to me, 'You will be okay. You will be okay.' When we got to the train station in Los Angeles, she went into a bathroom stall and shot herself. (*Long pause*) She killed herself while I was right outside. (*Long pause*) I grew up with an uncle and aunt who lived out there, but I never recovered. I cannot deal with any type of emotion at all. I just have to get away."

It is easy for us to get angry at the father's irresponsible emotional neglect of his daughter until we hear the story of his emotional trauma with his mother. Indeed, the father's failure is understandable, and we can easily see how his damage is related to how he damaged his daughter. His actions with his daughter have more to do with his mother's suicide than with how he feels about the daughter's competence. It becomes a little more difficult to hold the father responsible for his actions when we know his story.

It is essential, however, that the father remain responsible for his actions with his daughter. We can understand the father's background and how it shaped his actions, but what he did was still wrong. The relational insult that he suffered does not justify his passing the damage on to his little girl. In order to keep himself together, to protect himself from emotions, he left his daughter out on a limb, assuming that she was unworthy and that something was wrong with her. The father knew that he was denying his daughter something essential when he withdrew. He knew something was wrong. My mother and father knew something was wrong when there was physical abuse. I knew that there was something wrong when I was unreasonable and demanding with my children. None of us intended to damage our children by our actions, but our failure to deal with our own hurt and pain, where it belonged, is where we were irresponsible. This father should have dealt with his emotional violation by working through the reasons and reality of what his mother did, and not by avoiding and walling himself off from emotions. My parents should have dealt with their own legacy of abuse with their own parents, and not by letting their emotional instability find its way into their relationship with their children. And I still have to struggle to keep the pain of my past where it belongs, not with my innocent children who are looking to me for love and nurture, but with my parents, who are still available for me to resolve the past. When we are victims of irresponsibility, we must place the guilt where it belongs and not on other relationships.

Just as in this situation, pain and relational traumas seldom originate with just one person in one generation. They are usually passed along through many generations. But if we fail to do the work necessary to hold the person who victimized us responsible for his or her actions, we have a tendency to victimize others. Victims become victimizers unless they resolve the issue with the person who hurt them. The work of forgiveness helps place this responsibility squarely where it belongs. It helps us keep the victimization of the past rightly between us and our abusers.

Thus both the victim and victimizer have an interest in making their relationship right. The victimizer has caused hurt and should take responsibility and correct things, if possible. The victim needs to work with the victimizer to keep the injustice and guilt focused on their relationship so that the injustice does not drive the victim to dealing with his or her pain in a destructive way. One of the most powerful aspects of restoration through overt forgiving is that it makes this mutual benefit work very open between victim and victimizer. It presents both the victim and the victimizer with the opportunity to confront pain, assign responsibility, and rebuild the love and trust between them. When it is successful, it holds the potential not only to heal the pain from the wrongs done, but also to provide the ability for both the victim and victimizer to pass along healthy attitudes to other relationships, such as those with friends, spouses, and children. Love and trust are restored and *us* becomes alive, contributing to the potential to make our other relationships more secure and sound.

Because both the victim and victimizer have an interest in making things better, overt forgiving can be initiated by either. Because both relational parties have a vested interest and responsibility, the process of forgiving also may be initiated by either. Overt forgiving does not automatically solve all the relational problems, but it does form the basis for forging mutual cooperation and trust in spite of the damaged relationship. In the work of restoration, the process of forgiveness cannot be accomplished alone. In overt forgiving, both parties must confront the absence of love and trust and find a way to walk away from the meeting somewhat restored to relational security.

"Real" Forgiving

It is unfortunate, but people often will use a disguise of forgiveness to cause more damage or to get back at someone who has caused them hurt. I have seen it many times when, at a meeting between victim and victimizer, one or the other will assume a self-justifying or defensive posture that hurts the other and makes real forgiveness impossible. For instance, consider this from a son who is supposedly "forgiving" his father for sexually abusing him as a child.

> "Sure, I forgive you. My life is ruined. I find it impossible to have a relationship with anyone. I am constantly confused and fearful. But I forgive you if it makes you feel better."

This man probably does wish that he could be released from the pain and forgive, but he certainly is not ready to do so. What he is doing is using the opportunity to forgive to burden his victimizer with the reality of his pain and to make it clear that he sees no escape from his "ruined" life. But it is not only victims who may use the overt forgiving session for destructive ends. Hear this response from a husband who was supposed to be asking forgiveness from his wife for the many affairs he has had over the years.

> "I do ask you to forgive me because there was no excuse for having relationships with other women. I should have had the courage to face you and divorce you, since I never felt fulfilled in our marriage. I take responsibility for not doing the right thing."

This man is not taking responsibility for the affairs and the damage that they caused to his marriage. Instead, he is using the opportunity to escape responsibility for the affairs and the hurt they have caused by pointing out that the marriage was always unsatisfying and that he should never have worked on the relationship at all. No restoration will take place in this relationship, only more and deeper hurt.

If forgiving is really going to take place in overt forgiving, both victim and victimizer must believe in the process. Both must view the effort as an opportunity to take responsibility for the hurt and damage. Both must be willing to try to put the relationship back on course. The victim and victimizer must see each other as valuable people who have the potential to be and act differently. Finally, both must accept that a better relationship is in store for them in the future. Without this integrity of intention, the overt forgiving process will cause further hurt and damage.

Step One: Time and Place

Overt forgiving has much to offer. It is like a baseball game when there are two outs in the bottom of the ninth, one run behind, a man on first, and you are up at bat. All the attention is on you, and there are high expectations for things to go right. For this reason, I usually think it is advisable for a lot of thinking to go into deciding a time and place for overt forgiving.

The first and most important thing to consider is who will participate. Most of the time, this will mean just the victim and victimizer; for instance, the husband and wife where there has been an affair or the father and daughter where there has been incest. But there are circumstances when others may be involved. Victims often find it helpful to have someone along as a support system as they try to work through the forgiveness process. I have known many women who take along a spouse or friend when confronting their sexual abusers. Seldom does the spouse or friend play a significant role in the meeting, but his or her presence helps the victim to feel that he or she is not alone. Likewise, many of us have been abused by more than one person. In my case, both of my parents were responsible for part of the abuse. Many choose to have all the parties who harmed them present during the forgiveness session, but I always caution people to be careful about how many people are added into the mix of a forgiveness session. As more people are added, there is more potential for one of them to be defensive and for the process to deteriorate. I chose, for instance, to have separate forgiveness talks with my mother and my father. This allowed me to focus on my relationship with each and the responsibility of each apart from the other. I have had most success with one, or perhaps two, victimizers meeting with a victim.

If you are a victim, you can have a forgiveness session on your own with the person or persons who abused you. But there is so much potential for defensiveness that many people choose to include a professional therapist, or at least someone trained in human relationships, to keep the process on track. I believe this is the correct approach. A therapist or outsider can look out for the interest of both the victim and victimizer, and ensure that no exploitation or blaming is taking place. If things deteriorate, a professional can stop the session before too much damage has taken place. Finally, an outside helper can keep in mind the goals of the overt forgiving session and move it along to achieve those goals. I have known many people who have done this overt forgiving themselves. Some have had good results, and some have not. You must decide whether your situation would warrant someone's guiding you through this process. However, my experience with overt forgiving tells me that an outside helper is invaluable. An overt forgiving session is often a one-shot proposition that is like nuclear fusion. There is a narrow parameter of how it can go right — and countless ways in which it can go wrong!

After you decide who will participate, you should decide where and when the meeting will take place. If you involve a professional, then utilize his or her office. If not, I always suggest that you set up a neutral spot where you and your abuser will meet: a house or office of a friend, rather than a familiar setting where one has more control than the other. In terms of time, I tell people to plan on about one and a half hours. Sometimes the session takes less and sometimes slightly more. However, if there is not progress in two hours, it is unlikely that the session is going to yield much benefit.

The invitation for a meeting can be initiated by either the victim or victimizer, but I have most often worked with the victim in setting up the session. I always suggest that you be straight and truthful concerning the intent of the meeting with the person with whom you are pursuing overt forgiving. Too often, people report being "ambushed" by a session, like this mother.

> "I was told by my eldest daughter that we were going to get together to reminisce. I get here and find out that the whole family is here along with you [the therapist] and that we are going to deal with the past. I feel ambushed!"

It is best to approach the other person calmly and with a truthful proposition. You do not have to go into detail, but you do need to make it honest. Such was the case with a woman who was setting up a forgiveness session with her father, who had molested her as a child.

> "I told him that many things have happened in the past that have affected me and that I wanted to meet with him with my therapist to try and resolve these things. I told him that my intention was to try to make our relationship better and to put some of it back together. Immediately he started asking me what I wanted to talk about. I said that I would want to talk about that in the session, but if he did not want to come, I did not want to get into it with him. I just kept re-emphasizing that my desire was to help our relationship, and he finally agreed to come."

The focus of a request to meet with your victimizer or victim needs to be on discussing the past and resolving issues so that the relationship can be helped. Some people will turn down this opportunity, but I have found that an overwhelming majority will take the chance to make things better. If you are involving a professional, such as a therapist, it can be helpful to have the victim or victimizer talk with the helper over the phone. This gives the professional the opportunity to explain how the session will proceed and how he or she will not let it deteriorate into a blaming or attack session. With these assurances, many people will agree to meet with their victims or victimizers to try to resolve past wrongs or pain.

Step Two: The Essential Elements of Overt Forgiving

After a session is scheduled between you and the person with whom you want to achieve overt forgiving, you must set up a plan. If you have no goals or clear direction for the meeting, you will tend to rehearse exactly what you want to say, but have little idea of how the interaction will go or what you want to happen. I prefer to have an idea of the essential elements that will be sought in overt forgiving. Remember, you are trying to effect a new covenant or contract for an old and damaging relationship.

In order to make this new covenant or contract a reality, at least three distinct goals concerning the past must be accomplished.

Agreement

No matter who initiates the meeting, both the victim and victimizer must come to some agreement about the specifics of the past violation and damage. If we remember something in the relationship that was destructive and our abuser does not remember it or denies it, we begin to question ourselves, or we assume that the abuser is seeking to damage us again. For instance, if a man remembers that as a boy his father always referred to him as worthless, but the father says that he never thought that nor would ever have said such a thing, there already is a hurdle of lack of trust between the two that cannot be negotiated.

Agreement between us and our victimizer means that we come to the crux of the violation and both are able to articulate what happened and what was wrong. This confirms for both the victim and victimizer that even though perceptions might be different, there is no misunderstanding regarding some sort of violation that caused damage and pain. This does not mean that agreement between the victim and victimizer on the details surrounding the violation is absolute. Many times we will forget important details or simply block unpleasant memories. If you insist on agreement on details and perceptions, then it is likely that someone will be defensive. Such is the case with a woman confronting her father concerning past sexual abuse.

DAUGHTER: You sexually abused me as a girl. You did it to me a lot. Every week until I was 13, you were at me.

FATHER: Some things were not right, but it just is not true that I abused you every week.

DAUGHTER: It is true. You were in my room every week and it ruined my life.

FATHER: I did things that were wrong, but I did not do it that often.

This conversation of accusation and defensiveness could go on endlessly without resolution. When I speak of agreement, however, I mean "ballpark" agreement, which simply means that you do not try to take the same perspective, but try to agree on the general violation. For instance, in the above case, I asked the daughter to hold back.

THERAPIST: The essence of the violation. What is the essence of the violation?

DAUGHTER: He sexually abused me.

THERAPIST: Then simply leave it there and say that to your father.

DAUGHTER: (*to father*) You sexually abused me when I was young and I am hurt and damaged because of it.

THERAPIST: (*to father*) Did you sexually abuse your daughter? (*father nods.*) Then tell that to your daughter.

FATHER: You are right. I sexually abused you and hurt you badly.

In this instance, the father and daughter did not agree on all of the details of the abuse, but they did agree on the crux of the abuse. This allowed them to move on with the important work of forgiveness without having to deal with every "dot and tittle" of the violation. Instead, they dealt with only the essential violation.

Especially in families where parents were the abusers, there may be great difficulty in remembering the specifics of an important violation. Remember, if you were abused as a child, from your perspective the abuse was scary, terrible, and massive. From an adult perspective, it may have not have seemed as large, and so some abusers actually may not remember their deeds. It is still possible to come to agreement in these cases if the abuser acknowledges that what is remembered by the victim could indeed have happened. Such was the case with a young man who remembered his father's flying into a rage and beating him because he could not tie his shoes as a boy.

"I told my dad my memory of the daily fear and dread of not knowing how to tie my shoes and how he would curse me and slap me when he had to tie them. I know that this went on for at least three weeks and it terrorized me. My dad listened, but when I finished, he said that he really didn't remember anything about it. But he did say to me that he realized that he was out of control many times and that he knows that he could have done something like that. He told me that he believed me and was sorry. Even though he didn't remember, I felt like he acknowledged what he did."

In cases like these, the agreement must focus on the violator's irresponsibility in many areas of life, but it still can have the effect of their coming to agreement that the violation occurred and that it was wrong. Agreement simply means that both relational parties recognize that a severe and meaningful violation transpired between them that caused unjust relational damage. Whether that agreement is in detail or a general outline, it still is agreement.

Acknowledgment

After reaching an agreement concerning the violation and the pain that it caused, we must seek acknowledgment of responsibility. Acknowledgment of this responsibility on the part of the wrongdoer is an absolute essential in the overt forgiving process. It allows the victim to cancel out his or her claim to the injustice and stops holding the wrongdoer responsible for the injustice. When the victimizer acknowledges that he or she unjustly damaged you and admits being responsible, he or she is taking a position of self-accountability and holding himself or herself responsible for the violation.

When we are innocent victims of someone's relational violation, we have a justified claim against that person. A son has every right to be angry at his alcoholic mother and is justified in his position that she should have taken care of him as a child, instead of vice versa. He is right to hold the mother accountable because she robbed him of his childhood. We do not want to let our violators off the hook because we are vengeful; we do not let them escape responsibility because we have been denied something that was ours. We hold them accountable because of our desire for justice. The transgressed must hold the transgressor accountable until the demand for justice is met.

Overt forgiving does not mean that we try to obliterate responsibility and accountability. Forgiveness only works if justice is served in some way. When we come to an agreement on the violation and our victimizer acknowledges his or her responsibility, he or she does not escape justice. Rather, we as the victims can release ourselves from holding the wrongdoer accountable and responsible. We do not have to hold the victimizers responsible because the victimizers who acknowledge accountability hold themselves responsible. This transfer of responsibility for justice from victim to victimizer is one of the most important aspects of overt forgiving and is often experienced by the victim as an emotional release. Take the story of a man years after he was betrayed by his wife, who had had an affair.

> "I always wanted her to pay for how she hurt me. I wanted her to feel as much emotional pain as I did. Last week, I saw her in an elevator and she asked if she could talk with me for a minute. We went to my office and she told me that she was wrong to have had the affair and knew that it caused me a lot of pain. She said that she knew that our marriage would not last, but that she was dead wrong to hurt me by having another relationship. She said that she wanted me to know that she hasn't felt right since. It was strange. Once she said what she did, all my anger and desire to see her hurt went away. I ended up telling her that it was time for both of us to get on with our lives."

Acknowledgment does confer responsibility for past violations, but it does not set the past right. In this sense, acknowledging responsibility does not achieve forgiveness. It does say that I did wrong and that I see the hurt that I caused, but it does not promise that I will live in a loving and trustworthy way in the future. Forgiveness, the restoration of love and trust, only takes place when our victimizers execute their obligation to care for and nurture us and we can engage in a secure give-and-take relationship.

Apology

Apology is not just saying you're sorry for the damaging actions. It is actually a promise. The old idea of repentance is helpful to me in understanding apology. To repent does not just mean to feel bad about a transgression. It actually means that I feel bad about what I have done, and so will take a 180-degree turn and do the opposite of what I did before. True apology is like repentance. It is not only being sorry, but also involves making a strong effort to do the opposite of the transgression. When someone has violated us in the area of love and trust, an apology is actually a promise to try to do loving and trustworthy things for us in the future. First, it overtly states that our abuser would erase our pain if possible. If the victimizer had it to do over again, he or she would do it differently. Second, it tells us at least covertly, that the future relationship will be different. Apology always serves well in satisfying the injustice. For example, this is a conversation between a woman and her mother, who had stood by silently while her husband sexually abused the daughter as a young girl.

DAUGHTER: The pain has been unbearable sometimes. Every time I am with you and your husband, I feel like he could do it to me all over again.

MOTHER: I don't know what was wrong with me then. You are right, I did know something was going on. I felt helpless and I left you on your own. I was so wrong and I am so sorry.

DAUGHTER: (*after several minutes*) I want to believe you. How can I believe you?

MOTHER: I guarantee you that I am different now. I will never hesitate to tell him where he is wrong. I will go home from here and tell him that I was wrong in not standing up to him then for what he was doing to you and that I will never make that mistake again.

DAUGHTER: *(after several minutes)* That would make me feel better. It feels like a burden rolling off of me.

MOTHER: Please forgive me.

DAUGHTER: I can and I do.

MOTHER: *(after an embrace of several minutes)* I also finally feel a burden rolling off of me.

Apology is a true apology only if it includes this different attitude toward the future. Often apologies are words of forgiveness that are used so carelessly that they have lost meaning. Many people have no intention of really apologizing, such as this father who had abused his children when they were younger.

"I am sorry for all the horrible things I did to you. I'm sorry for being who I am and just trying to provide a good home and background for you kids. I am sorry for being such a failure."

This father probably has no intention of making his relationships with his children any different. Instead, he probably will harbor rage against them for even bringing up the subject of the past abuse, and will act in such a way that will make life more painful for the children. When words of an apology are spoken, but there is no intent to live differently, we should reject the apology and continue to hold the wrongdoer responsible for his or her actions. Only when a victimizer promises or lives differently can forgiveness and restoration take place.

Step Three: Accept the Apology and Forgive

If you can get through the labyrinth of agreement, acknowledgment, and apology without the overt forgiving session being blaming and defensive, then you really are in the home stretch.

Nothing is left but for you and your victimizer to consummate the desire to live in a trustworthy and loving way and to put the past behind. But human beings are unpredictable. After living with the effects of our abuse and violations for many years, we may have a difficult time believing what we have seen take place in the forgiving session. We want to believe that something meaningful and life-changing has happened, but because of our past, we instead think that we imagined the importance of such a session. In order to help along the process of forgiving and ensure that the work of forgiveness can be remembered, I find it helpful to have the victim and victimizer engage in forgiveness rituals. Rituals are extremely powerful because they combine our actions with specific meanings. Usually the actions are out of the ordinary enough to make a distinct impression on us. Then, when we remember the distinctive action, we remember the meaning of the action, and it helps us realize the full potential and impact of ritualistic acts. In overt forgiving, most of the rituals I suggest will heighten the experience of acknowledgment, apology, or forgiving.

The particular ritual that is performed may vary from situation to situation, but it is important to remember that the ritual must be important to both the forgiver and forgiven. In situations where the violation has been severe but much time has passed since it took place, I have suggested that the two relational parties try to recall as many specific details of the violation as possible work and then choose items that represent the trauma. The presence of these items brings the situation and violation closer to both the victim and wrongdoer, and acknowledgment of the injustice is facilitated. For example, the following is from a case where a man had had an adulterous affair years before his wife found out about it. He was asked to bring something that would represent the affair.

MAN: I thought and thought about what this woman meant to me, but all I really kept coming up with was the sexual relationship and all the money I spent keeping the affair going. I paid all the ex-

	penses with a separate credit card so I wouldn't get caught. I brought along the credit card and all of the credit card bills for the three years I had the affair.
WOMAN:	Does that represent what she meant to you?
MAN:	I'm not sure what she meant to me. I find myself denying that the affair was all that bad. I pretend that it didn't take anything away from you. But when I'm faced with the amount of money that I spent on her, I can't deny that I stole from you and gave to her. More than just financially, too.

Many things can be used to bring the presence of the wrong into the session and make the impact of acknowledgment greater, including photos, mementos, clothing, or toys. Anything will work if it helps you to connect with the injustice.

In the work of overt forgiving, victims sometimes find it difficult to view the victimizers as really sorry and repentant concerning the past actions. Sometimes the victimizers themselves have a difficult time acknowledging regret for those actions. In cases such as these, I usually recommend a ritual that shows physically that the victimizer feels hurt for damaging the victim. Again, these rituals may include any action or symbol, but they are designed to help the victimizer reckon with the gravity of his or her violation and to help the victim clearly recognize and accept the apology of the victimizer. I use many rituals, but the one I suggest most often is for the transgressor to get on his or her knees when making the apology and asking for forgiveness. This is a religious symbol, but I find that it is hard for a victimizer not to be humble when on his or her knees and very difficult for the victim not to recognize the victimizer's sincerity. Such was the case with a father who got down on his knees to apologize to his wife for beating her.

MAN:	I know how I have hurt you and I am sorry. I promise to get the help I need and never hit you again.

WOMAN: (*clearly surprised*) I can't believe you are on your
            knees. I didn't think you would do that for any-
            one, especially me.

MAN: I didn't think I would either. It sure makes me re-
            alize, though, that this is where I should have been
            a long time ago. I am sorry for what I've done. I
            really do want you to forgive me, if you can.

WOMAN: It is hard. I didn't think I could. But if you're will-
            ing to get on your knees, you must be serious. I
            will try to forgive you.

Some of us will need to participate in a ritual to assure ourselves our victimizer recognizes how he or she has hurt us. Many
such rituals focus on the victimizer's suffering a little humiliation
to show us that there is a clear understanding of how he or she
humiliated us or how we suffered at his or her hands. I usually
suggest that people who have victimized someone choose their
own symbol of "penance." One man chose to shave his head to
show how sorry he was for lying about his wife to other family
members, telling them that she was having extramarital affairs.

MAN: I shaved my head to say I was serious and was really
            sorry for what I said about my wife. Of course, every-
            one assumed as soon as they saw me that I was being
            treated for cancer. When they asked me what was
            wrong, I told them the truth. I didn't have cancer. I
            lied about my wife, and was showing that I was sorry
            and was grieving about what I had done.

WOMAN: I can tell you that I didn't believe him at first. But the
            more he told people and owned up to what he did, I
            could see that he was really willing to admit responsi-
            bility. That is a hard thing to do. It did help me be-
            lieve him.

When the victim is ready to give forgiveness, it is sometimes
helpful to incorporate a ritual that symbolizes the end of the old

relationship and the beginning of a new one. I often suggest that the symbols of the transgression that were used in the acknowledgment be gotten rid of in some ritualistic fashion, such as by burning or burying them. For example, in the example of the man who had brought in his credit card and bills, after forgiveness was achieved, the couple burned the plastic and paper in the fireplace. Some couples, after forgiving an affair, will have a remarriage ritual, in which they restate their vows of fidelity to each other and place rings on each other's fingers. In one case, a mother and daughter used various objects, such as a charm bracelet, a small necklace, and a small stuffed animal to represent the daughter's lost childhood, when the girl was used by her mother in an adult way to fulfill her own desires and dreams. After the daughter forgave the mother for manipulating and misusing her, she suggested that they put the objects in a jar and bury them in the mother's backyard. I said that since they were burying the past, when they wanted to rehash the abuse, they could dig up the jar and rebury it when they were through. A year later, the daughter reported:

> "It was so helpful for me to bury those things and have the agreement that we would dig them up if we needed to talk. Every time I started to think about the past and start feeling the pain, I would remind myself that we had worked through that stuff, and if I needed to go back, I would ask Mom to dig up the jar. That would remind me that I had forgiven her and that my mother was sorry. I never had to dig up the jar."

It is important to remember that just because we forgive does not mean that we will not ever feel the pain again. Forgiving does not mean forgetting. We cannot erase the memories of violation and abuse. Forgiveness simply means that we can move past the pain of the injustice, but every now and again, it will come back to bite us. In my case, I had worked through much of the pain of my past abuse and really had forgiven my parents. However, when I saw a movie that had a quite explicit scene of a young boy being abused, I found myself unable to sleep and becoming more and more depressed. I would engage in long and unproductive thoughts about how unfair my own abuse had been and how angry I was that my life was not different. I became dissatisfied with my job and was despondent in my family — much like I had been before I started working on my issues with my parents.

Was my work of forgiveness all a lie? Not really. I was just experiencing the backwash of the pain and memories through an inadvertent trigger. When I confronted my thoughts of the abuse with the reality of the forgiveness that had happened between me and my parents, I started to recapture lost ground and soon surpassed the old self. I still come across scenes in books or movies or songs that prompt this backwash. That is to be expected, but I can deal with it if I remind myself of the good work of forgiveness already accomplished.

OVERT FORGIVING AND THE WORK OF FORGIVENESS

For many, overt forgiving in a face-to-face conversation between the victim and victimizer is the only work that can satisfy their need for confrontation and possible forgiveness. For these people, the desire to deal with the past violations in a "once-and-for-all" fashion is the driving force. Indeed, I have seen many cases where overt forgiving accomplished in a few hours what I would have considered a year's worth of work. I have seen victim and victimizer leave sessions arm-in-arm, united and secure in their desire to live their relationship better. In many cases of overt forgiving, the new relationship is much closer than the one that existed before the damage occurred. However, negotiation of the maze that includes the three elements of agreement, acknowledgment, and apology can be treacherous and opens up many opportunities for relational deterioration. We must be aware that no matter how badly we want a session to go well, it may result in defensiveness, accusations, and counter accusations. With all of the positive potential of overt forgiving in relationships, it can also cause more damage and hurt.

With this much risk, why pursue overt forgiving at all? This is a wise question. Overt forgiving is not appropriate in all situations and is certainly not for everyone, especially when we still have tremendous pain or have not learned some of the lessons of forgiveness in the other stations. However, many will say that nothing less than overt forgiving will do. You may feel that you can never even consider doing the work of forgiveness with a victimizer until you see that the wrongdoer realizes the pain and takes responsibility. In these cases, overt forgiving serves as the initial effort in building future trustworthiness. You may believe that if you do not engage in face-to-face overt forgiving, the work of forgiveness will always seem false or fake. You may just believe that any work of forgiveness will be incomplete in terms of your own healing unless the past is overtly confronted. All of these are valid reasons to pursue this station of forgiveness, and the risk that is taken in achieving relational restoration may be well worth the rewards.

But whether overt forgiving is used as the starting place in the work of forgiveness or the ending place, it involves a never-ending journey of learning to live in more responsible, loving, and trustworthy relationships. Overt forgiving works best when we look for insight in doing our part responsibly in the give-and-take of relating, understanding the humanness of our victimizer, and committing ourselves to doing better. My wife has a saying, "It's a long life." It is a long life, although we might have difficulty now recognizing the possibilities in the work of forgiveness that may change later on. If we hang in there, we can get the work of forgiveness done.

Special Focus Eight:
Working on Overt Forgiving

1. What are some of the reasons why you think overt forgiving is right for this relationship?

2. Who could serve as a helper to you in preparing for a forgiveness session? Talk through details with this person and be patient in setting the right time.

3. Rehearse or roleplay with someone how you would invite the person with whom you want to effect forgiveness to a session.

4. Think about how the interaction will take place in the session. What are some of the pitfalls you need to be careful to avoid?

5. Roleplay or think about the goals of overt forgiving in terms of agreement, acknowledgment, and apology.

Special Focus Nine:
Where Are You in the Stations of Forgiveness?

Directions: Rate the following statements as they apply to you. Because each person is unique, there are no right or wrong answers. Just try to respond as honestly as you can. Please respond to every statement.

After reading each statement, check the answer that BEST describes the way you feel or act.

1. This person has apologized to me for the pain he or she has caused in my life.

___ Yes, I believe this is true.
___ No, I believe this is false.

2. I believe we are on the road to restoring our relationship.

___ Yes, I believe this.
___ No, I seldom feel this way.

3. I have a current relationship with this person and feel little need to talk about the past hurt.

___ Yes, this is mostly true.
___ No, this is mostly false.

4. I believe this person would not intentionally hurt me again because he or she is now trustworthy in our relationship.

___ Yes, this is true.
___ No, this is hardly ever true.

5. The only way I can deal with this relationship is to keep my distance from this person.

___ Yes, this is mostly true.
___ No, this is mostly false.

6. My relationship with this person has improved gradually over time by just being together and having mostly good times.

___ Yes, this is mostly true.
___ No, this is mostly false.

7. I feel powerless over the circumstances of our relationship when I'm with this person.

___ Yes, I feel this way.
___ No, I do not feel this way.

8. I have difficulty in stopping this person from causing me hurt.

___ Yes, I have this difficulty.
___ No, this is mostly not the case.

9. This person has pain that has nothing to do with me.

___ Yes, I am sure this is true.
___ No, I do not believe this is true.

10. Things are not completely resolved in our relationship, but it is getting better.

___ Yes, this is mostly true.
___ No, this is mostly false.

11. I have trouble sorting out my emotions with regard to this person.

___ Yes, I have this trouble often.
___ No, I am clear on my feelings.

12. This person acknowledges that he or she has done things wrong in the past concerning our relationship.

___ Yes, this is mostly true.
___ No, this is mostly false.

13. I never seem to "win" when it comes to relating to this person.

___ Yes, this is mostly true.
___ No, this is mostly untrue.

14. When this person is cruel to me, it has more to do with his or her problems than it does with me.

___ Yes, I believe this.
___ No, I do not believe this.

15. For the most part, I deserve the things that have happened to me.

___ Yes, most of the time.
___ No, I do not believe this.

16. I know how to effectively stop this person from causing me pain.

___ Yes, most of the time.
___ No, almost never.

17. This person has taken responsibility for causing me pain.

___ Yes, I believe this.
___ No, I do not believe this.

18. I understand why I feel pain from this person.

___ Yes, it is fairly clear to me.
___ No, I am fairly confused.

19. Our relationship is improving a little each time we are together.

___ Yes, I find this mostly true.
___ No, this is mostly false.

20. If I had come from this person's background, I might do some harmful things to people.

___ Yes, I might have.
___ No, I would have done better.

21. When I talked to this person about the damage he or she caused, he or she accepted responsibility.

___ Yes, for the most part.
___ No, he or she mostly did not.

22. I believe that our relationship is making progress and some-day may be totally healed.

___ Yes, I believe this.
___ No, I seldom feel this way.

Scoring of the IRRS

The statements you have just completed are from the *Forgiveness Scale* of the IRRS (Hargrave & Sells, 1997) and it gives an idea of where you are in the work of forgiveness using the subscales of *insight, understanding, giving the opportunity for compensation,* and *overt forgiving.*

Insight
  Insight is the ability to recognize transactional patterns and

mechanisms by which relational damage was perpetrated and interrupt or intervene in the patterns to prevent relational damage in the future. High scores (8 or above) may indicate that a person would experience confusion concerning emotional pain and would be unable to make specific statements regarding painful interactions or how to avoid them. Low scores (6 or below) may indicate clarity in identifying pain and knowing how to avoid painful interactions.

Understanding

Understanding is the ability to make personal identification with the position, limitations, development, efforts, and intent of the person who caused relational damage. High scores (8 or above) may indicate that the person either blames himself or herself or the perpetrator to an unreasonable degree without consideration of context or circumstances. Low scores (6 or below) may indicate that a person clearly understands the circumstances that must be considered in determining responsibility for relational deterioration.

Giving the Opportunity for Compensation

Giving the Opportunity for Compensation is the ability to engage in interactions and relationships with the former perpetrator in a way that is perceived by the victim as nonthreatening and builds emotional bonding. High scores (13 or above) may indicate that a person views a continued relationship with the perpetrator as non-trustworthy and that interactions are marked with communications that cause pain. Low scores (10 or below) may indicate that a person perceives that he or she is able to engage in a relationship with the perpetrator that promotes reasonable care and desires to continue the relationship in the future.

Overt Forgiving

Overt Forgiving is the perceived ability of a person to discuss past relational damage with the perpetrator and resolve issues of responsibility for specific violations to the point where the relationship can be secure and trustworthy. High scores (9 or above) may indicate that a person perceives himself or herself as unable to discuss or unsuccessful in discussing and resolving the relational damage. Low scores (7 or below) may indicate that a person perceives himself or herself as successful in overtly discussing the relational damage with the perpetrator and that a greater sense of trust resulted from the discussion.

Add the following together:

INSIGHT *score*

7. 2 for Yes, 1 for No   ____
8. 2 for Yes, 1 for No   ____
11. 2 for Yes, 1 for No   ____
16. 1 for Yes, 2 for No   ____
18. 1 for Yes, 2 for No   ____

        TOTAL: ____

UNDERSTANDING *score*

9. 1 for Yes, 2 for No
13. 2 for Yes, 1 for No   ____
14. 1 for Yes, 2 for No   ____
15. 2 for Yes, 1 for No   ____
20. 1 for Yes, 2 for No   ____

        TOTAL: ____

GIVING THE OPPORTUNITY FOR COMPENSATION *score*

2. 1 for Yes, 2 for No   ____
3. 1 for Yes, 2 for No   ____
5. 2 for Yes, 1 for No   ____
6. 1 for Yes, 2 for No   ____

10. 1 for Yes, 2 for No   ___
19. 1 for Yes, 2 for No   ___
22. 1 for Yes, 2 for No   ___

          TOTAL: ___

OVERT FORGIVING score

1. 1 for Yes, 2 for No   ___
4. 1 for Yes, 2 for No   ___
12. 1 for Yes, 2 for No   ___
17. 1 for Yes, 2 for No   ___
21. 1 for Yes, 2 for No   ___

          TOTAL: ___

Section Three

Questions Concerning the Work of Forgiveness

7

Some Questions and Final Thoughts

Forgiveness is sloppy and messy work at best. What I have tried to do in this book is outline a framework that has been helpful to some people in conceptualizing a way to go about moving past the old relationships that have caused them so much pain. But it is important to remember that you may choose not to forgive. I believe in the power of forgiveness and its curative factors with regard to the human psyche and relationships, but I would never state that you must forgive the wrong done to you. It is an individual choice and you do not have to justify that choice to anyone. Likewise, this is not the only model from which to pursue the work of forgiveness. I am pragmatic enough to believe that there are many ways to achieve forgiveness, and if a way works for you and makes you and your relationships better, it qualifies and gets a vote of confidence from me.

But the work of forgiveness in the model that I have outlined has been helpful to many. It is a process-oriented model that allows you to move back and forth among the stations of insight, understanding, giving the opportunity for compensation, and overt forgiving in appropriate ways in different relationships. The stations are varied enough to provide a reasonable way for all people to pursue some healing related to forgiveness. It is also a model that emphasizes responsibility, and not just grace. In this aspect,

I find the model justice-based and realistic in protecting people from future harm. Finally, it is systemic in that it not only takes into account the interests and trauma of the victim, but also recognizes the past and limitations of the victimizer.

I do many seminars based on this framework and always encourage questions. You may have similar ones. Here are some of the most common questions I have been asked over the years.

What is the right station at which to begin the work of forgiveness?

The correct answer is that there is no "right" first station. The stations are free-flowing, and most often people will find one that feels appropriate to the work that they are ready to do at a particular time. Some will start out with the work in insight, do a little in giving the opportunity for compensation, move to understanding, get a little more insight, do more giving the opportunity for compensation, and so on, and find that forgiveness involved many of the stations. Others will start with overt forgiving, only to go back and rework the other three stations.

However, if you do not know where to begin, I always suggest that the safe bet is doing the work of salvage first. Salvage in insight and understanding does much good in easing your pain and helping you to recognize destructive patterns. It also can be done with no relational risk because you do not have to expose yourself to the victimizer. In this way, it provides some benefits of forgiveness with little risk. If you do not know where to begin, I suggest that you begin there.

How does one go about the work of forgiveness when the perpetrator is gone or has died?

In the model that I have outlined, salvage through insight and understanding provides a dynamic and important way to achieve forgiveness. Insight allows us to identify how we were damaged and the mechanisms and actions that caused that damage. When we recognize these interactions and patterns, we can stop others from using them to hurt us and stop ourselves from using them to hurt others. Understanding helps us identify with the history, limitations, roles, and situations that faced our abusers. When we recognize our own fallibility in the face of our victimizer's situation, we usually realize that he or she was a person, just like us, that made some bad and irresponsible choices. This helps us move past the heavy burden of shame, rage, over-control, or highly chaotic behavior that causes us great pain. Salvage makes us better people because we do not feel as much pain, and makes us better relational partners because we do not engage in or tolerate destructive patterns. Trust and love are restored to some relationships, and thus a degree of forgiveness is achieved.

Salvage work is always available in doing forgiveness work with a person who has left or who died. We can review patterns in the past to achieve insight, and understanding can be attained through our own research or by talking with members of our violator's family. Salvage does not require contact with the person who harmed us.

However, there is no possibility of restoration. I believe that restoration means putting the old and damaged relationship back into working order where it is loving and trustworthy. There is no way to restore a relationship with a person who is dead. In such cases, the work of salvage is the only alternative.

Some people say "forgive and forget." Is this right?

Forgiving does not mean forgetting. Forgiving means that we remember everything about how we were damaged by our abusers. But we confront the damage, and the damager, and seek to learn how to prevent our being damaged in the future. We look at his or her personhood and see him or her as a human who makes mistakes instead of as a monster who was unreasoning in violating us. We are realistic as to how we can move the relationship to a position where we can regain a sense of love and trust. And we are open to the possibility of releasing our justified right to hold the violation over the head of the violator when he or she is willing to hold himself or herself responsible. We do not, and should not, forget when we forgive. One of the most beautiful things about forgiveness is that I can look squarely at the damage and the person who caused it and then say, I forgive.

When we are really able to forgive, we can forget that we have to hold someone responsible for our pain. Most people experience this as a release, and it is helpful in moving on with their lives. Also, much of the pain that is associated with the past tends to subside after forgiveness. This is not the same as "forgetting," but it does mean that the pain and judgement becomes less and less familiar.

Is there a time where family damage is so severe that forgiveness is not appropriate?

I am afraid that the answer is "Yes." This indeed is a terrible thing, but I have seen situations and family members so destructive that no one could gain enough insight into the patterns that caused the destruction to undo them. The victimizer seemed to consistently choose to hurt others. These acts may represent a personality disorder, and certainly a damaged past, but that should not vindicate the person's desire to hurt the family.

In situations like these, the best and only insight available to us is to isolate ourselves from the violator. It is much like the Chernobyl nuclear reactor site. The nuclear core of the damaged reactor is still active and dangerous. It was encased in acres and acres of concrete, but its radioactivity still seeps out into the surrounding area. Little can be done but to wait for the danger to subside. But how long will we have to wait? In the case of Chernobyl, beyond our lifetimes. The potential for damage is so great, and our understanding so limited, that we cannot stop the damage. In cases where a family member continues to cause great damage, sometimes the best we can do is pull back and not sacrifice ourselves to more and more violations.

If you have been exposed to a family member who is this dangerous, however, you should be aware of your own destructive tendencies. Certainly you can learn to live and love in productive relationships with family and friends, but you have been unjustly damaged, and that insult leaves you in a position to potentially play out your injustice in a destructive way. If you isolate yourself from a damaging family member, you need to continually check yourself and your interactions in relationships to make sure that you do not take out your exploitation on someone else.

How can a people, such as the Jews, ever be expected to
forgive an atrocity like the Holocaust?

Most second- and third-generation Jews to whom I have talked do not see it as their responsibility to forgive the Holocaust. Only the people who were victims of the Holocaust have the right to forgive. Most Jews today feel that their responsibility is to never forget, and to make sure that it never happens again.

Certainly, I feel that people must make their own decisions concerning forgiveness. But I do believe that the Jews have done some of the work of forgiveness already. Most survivors of the Holocaust resisted the temptation to retaliate. They did not talk very much about their experiences, but did the best they could to raise their families to be "normal." Many bore the burden of this crime against humanity by trying to do their family good and by not seeking revenge. The next generation, from my observation, has tried to make sense of the family experience, and again, not retaliate. I believe that the first and second generations of survivors have been involved the work of insight. They have made remarkable strides in recognizing the damage done to them and not committing those same acts themselves.

Perhaps in two or three more generations, we will see Jews experiment with understanding their former persecutors, and some even engaging in giving the opportunity for compensation. I believe that this is the process of forgiveness among cultures, and even in families, where there has been horrendous abuse. It takes generations, but reconciliatory acts can occur. This is the type of reconciliation we can hope for between Palestinians and Jews and the people of Bosnia. These groups can be retaliatory and destructive, but the potential is there for slow and sequential steps that could culminate in forgiveness.

Can or should one forgive a person who has never
taken responsibility for the damage he or she has caused
and refuses to apologize?

The work of forgiveness is imperfect at best. We can never really know the heart of another individual and feel totally secure about that person taking responsibility for his or her past actions. The best we can do is judge what they say and compare it with what they do. From this information, we make our relational decision concerning our own level of giving and vulnerability.

If a person is truly unrepentant and will not acknowledge responsibility for his or her actions, then forgiveness through restoration is not possible. There is still forgiveness through salvage, but I would offer one caution here. Many times people do not acknowledge responsibility because of the way in which they perceive the past. For instance, my mother claimed to be a good mother even though she physically abused her children. Compared with her abusive father, however, she was indeed a good mother. If I approached the proviso of forgiveness with the idea that I wanted her to take responsibility for being a terrible parent, she probably would not acknowledge responsibility. It is necessary to weed the perceptions of victim and victimizer carefully before we are sure that a victimizer is unwilling to acknowledge any responsibility.

Doesn't your model make the victim responsible for
solving the violation in the station of insight?

There is an aspect of this that is true. In the station of insight, I do suggest to victims that they provide a detailed sequence of the actions and patterns that led to the violation. I then ask the victims to make adjustments in their patterns and actions that will force the victimizers to change their patterns or actions. In a way, I can see how it could be ascertained that since I am giving the responsibility for change to the victim, I am making him or her at least partially responsible for the abuse.

I am a systemic therapist. Because of that, I believe that a change in one part of the system has the potential, through its interaction, to change another part of the system. I see this as a necessary part of relating. I do not believe that victims are responsible for their own abuse, but I do believe that they participate in a system that will allow them to manage some of the power of the relationship and take responsibility for protecting themselves. So, the responsibility that deals with insight is not about guilt, but about gaining the power to protect yourself from damaging relationships.

Do you believe that victimizers ever really change?
Can they ever be trusted?

Humans are not perfect. No person is ever totally trustworthy and loving. When I say that I trust my wife, it is not because she has never done anything that hurt me. Indeed, she has hurt me, and I her. What I mean is that the hurt that she does cause me through violations is more than compensated by the way she is consistently trustworthy, supportive, and loyal. This allows me, *in the long run,* to count on her being there when I need her and to give to me freely.

When we are trying to restore a broken relationship with someone who has hurt us, we are not looking for perfection. We are looking for, on average, a person who will love and nurture us more often and consistently enough that we can once again consider that person trustworthy. Do I believe that past violators can become trustworthy people? Absolutely. I see people make these courageous changes all the time, and have experienced it myself in my life.

Most of your examples are from a victim's perspective.
Does the process of forgiveness work in a similar way
for a victimizer?

Yes. As I have stated before, most victimizers are also victims. Once you victimize someone, you have a special insight into what it feels like from both perspectives. The key element in the work of forgiveness is the desire to make sure that the relationship will not hurt any more. If you are a victimizer, you certainly do qualify as wanting a healthy relationship. I find that many of my clients wish to reconcile and restore old broken relationships in which they caused damage. I would offer a few cautions, however, to victimizers seeking forgiveness.

First, the victimizer should move at the desired pace of the victim. The victimizer was responsible for the transgression and has no claim on the victim to "have to engage in forgiveness." Sometimes victimizers try too hard, and victims experience their desire for forgiveness as controlling, demanding, or manipulative. If the victim needs time, the victimizer should express a desire and willingness to take responsibility, and then let the victim dictate the schedule. Second, the victimizer should make sure that if he or she seeks forgiveness, real change is going to occur. This change must be governed by how our victim believes we need to change and not how we assume we need to change. For relational progress and restoration to take place, we must listen to our victims and make sure that we do not hurt them again. Rather than asking for forgiveness directly, it is often much more helpful for the victimizer to compensate the victim through current responsible giving and to *prove* trustworthiness. This places actions before words, and often helps the victim to give more credence to our desire for overt forgiveness.

Is self-forgiveness possible?

My premise for forgiveness is that people are hurt by relationships and need to be healed by relationships. When people talk about the need to forgive the self, I most often think that they are referring to the pain that an individual suffers through being a victim or victimizer. The relationships that we counted on are very powerful in their ability to program us concerning our beliefs about who we are and how we are to behave. The beliefs about ourselves do not come from ourselves, however; they come from our experiences in relationships. So most of the time I feel that self-forgiveness is really about finding out where we stand as a victim or victimizer in our current and past relationships, and going about the work of forgiveness in those relationships.

Sometimes I'm asked: "Can't you have a relationship with yourself?" Maybe. At this point, however, I do not see clearly how a person could relate to himself or herself, and so I do not see forgiveness of self as an essential function. Nevertheless, I am a pragmatist. If someone were to tell me that he or she forgave himself or herself and there was a release of old feelings that resulted in the ability to relate to others better, I would encourage the experience.

I may want to work toward overt forgiveness in my family,
but my siblings are not willing to reveal the family secrets.
How can I deal with this situation?

I remember very clearly how, in my own family, when I decided to work on the past abuse with my parents, I asked all of my siblings to become involved in the work. My sister and my two brothers all turned me down. Basically, it boiled down to the fact that they did not want to dig up all that "stuff" in our family past. I could not really blame them, but it left me feeling alone.

In situations where one sibling wants to pursue overt forgiving and the other does not, often the family defensiveness will result in everyone's forming a coalition that excludes the one seeking overt forgiving. This "us" against "them" position often leads to further polarization as the victim becomes more and more insistent about the problems of the family while other family members staunchly maintain that there is, in fact, nothing wrong. In these situations, if you are the one who is excluded, you might want to go back and do work in the first three stations of forgiveness. These efforts do not require you to discuss anything openly with defensive family members. As you achieve some benefits from your work, that may affect the family group in the long run, and eventually you may get to overt forgiving. If you can take each family member aside separately and discuss the issues of forgiveness, it may be possible to avoid the family's establishing a defensive coalition against you.

Another way in which this issue may be confronted is by anger and resentment on the part of siblings who do not want you to forgive abusive family members. They may feel that if you forgive, you will desert the others. In abusive families, adult siblings often form a solid coalition against relationally irresponsible siblings or parents. If you pursue the work of forgiveness and are successful in restoring the relationship, the sibling coalition can be broken up. You may, as a result, find yourself in a situation of split loyalty, where being forgiving of a past abusive relationship means that you are being disloyal to a formerly close family member. The best suggestion in this case is for you and your sibling to talk openly about your desire for reconciliation. Assure him or her that you will not desert the relationship, but that you need to seek restoration. Invite the sibling to explore it with you, but do not be surprised if he or she turns down the offer. The fact is that if you are successful, you probably will find that even close relationships will become more distant if you forgive and your sibling does not. However, remember that it is a long life and these relationships may find a way to reform without your trying to make it happen.

What about the false memory syndrome? Don't many
people who think they have violations in their pasts
just "create" those memories?

The so-called false memory syndrome has been one of the hotter topics in the media over the past several years. There is a real fear concerning false memories, and for good reason. Research suggests that we can indeed create memory. I believe that the brain is designed to make sense out of the world. If you ask it a question, it will try to answer you. If you have some very vague and non-specific memories of being in a dark place, scared and alone, you may wonder whether they may not represent some repressed memory of past abuse. If you continue to focus on the vague memory, your mind will likely start creating little pieces of explanations that will fit with the memory. Along with your interpretation, you might actively engage in memory construction. Of course, none of this memory may be true; it was created because you asked your brain to explain some vague feelings and your brain tried to answer. Many therapists have been well-meaning accomplices in this practice by encouraging clients to mull over disturbing but non-specific feelings related to the past.

I believe there are true repressed memories. But I find that, in my practice, when someone remembers a repressed memory, he or she remembers it in big chunks at a time. When these types of memories come, they almost never are about the things on which the client has been focusing. They are inspired by a situation or material that cues something that has been repressed for years. I believe that these types of memories are reliable.

We must be cautious with our memories. We are all familiar with stories of families that were devastated because of unsupported accusations based on possible "false" memory. But we do need to take seriously a person's memory and perceptions, especially when those memories include abuse or violations. Whether these memories are real or perceived, they are still in need of healing.

Is there a place for revenge?

Revenge is a popular theme for movies. We see "First Wives Club" or "Waiting to Exhale" and cheer when the hero strikes back at the persecutor. In reality, however, revenge seldom makes the situation better. First, revenge is almost always based in anger. It moves past just trying to protect ourselves from exploitation into wanting to see the person who hurt us suffer. Cognitively, we consider taking the same type of destructive action as the one that hurt us. Second, revenge almost never renders the victimizer helpless. Unlike in the movies, once we strike out in revenge, the person who hurt us originally is likely to try to hurt us again. This leads to an escalation of violence that leaves us with more damage than that for which we bargained. Finally, revenge tears down relationships and leaves little room for building and restoring them. On a philosophical level, I want to be remembered as a person who built relationships, and not as one of whom others were fearful.

Doesn't forgiveness let the wrongdoer off the hook?

I believe this is a common fear among professionals in my field. The person who has done the wrong in the relationship seemingly gets off without a scratch, and the victim has to be the one to forgive. I do not believe that forgiveness by a victim necessitates that he or she allow himself or herself to be exposed to a situation where there is violation and hurt. You can, and should, take steps to protect yourself from people who are irresponsible. That is what insight is all about. I also do not believe that forgiveness means that the victimizer just walks away. If true forgiveness takes place, the victimizer takes the responsibility for his or her guilty actions from the shoulders of the victim. In addition, the victimizer carries the burden of now proving himself or herself a loving and trustworthy person. Most professionals who are against the idea of forgiveness assume that it means that the victimizer will have no responsibility, and that the victims will be hurt again by the same person. Real forgiveness does not allow such things to happen.

I am a Christian, and Jesus said that if we do not forgive others, God will not forgive us. How does this fit with your framework?

Many of the world religions discuss the need and obligation to give and receive forgiveness. In order to answer the question correctly, you must look at the whole of Jesus' life. It is true that he said, "If you do not forgive others, God will not forgive you." I become disturbed, however, when I see how Jesus treated the religious scholars of his day. He certainly did not appear to be forgiving of them. Did he violate his own command?

I think not. When I think of Jesus, I think of his doing the work of redemption during his entire ministry. I feel that he did this work of redemption on the level where people were ready to restore their relationship with God. Therefore, in the case of the disciples, he was redemptive by joining with them and telling them to become his followers. With the woman at the well, he was redemptive by telling her that he was willing to give her another chance to act in trustworthy ways. And in the case of the religious leaders, I believe he was redemptive by setting them a clear boundary that did not tolerate their misuse of religion and demanded a change of heart and of action. Even when Jesus is stern and appears to be condemning, I believe he is using his insight to stop the destructive interactions of those who would use their relationship with God to be exploitative. Everything he did was about restoration and forgiveness.

In the same way, there is more than one way to forgive in our relationships. Sometimes the most forgiving thing we can do is to set firm boundaries so that people cannot exploit and misuse our relationship. Sometimes forgiveness will involve our making an identification with the people who do us wrong. At still other times, the forgiving thing to do is to look someone who has harmed us in the eye and say, "I forgive you." Jesus is one of the examples of forgiveness that I use to illustrate the different stations of forgiveness. Believing that forgiveness just involves mimicking words does not seem to follow the example of Jesus.

Some Final Thoughts
on the Work of Forgiveness

How do we forgive? Slowly. Thoughtfully. Quickly. Spontaneously. A little at a time. All at once. The ways in which people will restore and salvage damaged and hurtful relationships will vary. I find it amazing that humans are able to do this work of forgiveness at all. But somehow, with all the variations of culture, gender, race, and background, people find a way to forgive even the most heinous of crimes.

Why do we forgive? This is perhaps a more difficult question to answer. I imagine that it has something to do with our need to survive. I am always struck by how little I know about my ancestors. The people who contributed to my genetic heritage are largely a mystery to me. I do not have any of their possessions. They did not leave me any money. I do not know the houses in which they lived. The best I can do is reach back three generations and name a few names. I do not know the people behind them.

The harder reality is that in two to three generations from now, no one in my family is likely to know me. I will have lived my life and I will die. Probably many of my "precious" possessions will have been lost, stolen, or broken. I doubt very seriously that I will have any significant amount of money to pass along, and even if I do, my family probably will not recognize me as the donor. I will be lost and gone, and no one will even know my name.

But there is something I can do that will provide a legacy that will last long past two or three generations to come. If I live my relationships in such a way that it builds other relationships with love and trust, then I will supply my lineage with a healthy dose of nourishment that will enable them to love and trust in their own relationships. Love and trust will make them strong, well-balanced, and giving. These future family members will be structured and influenced by the way in which I participate in the relationships that are relevant to me. It is like a cable that runs from my past through me to the future. If I do my part in keeping the cable in good repair and strengthening it now, it will be better able to support the future burdens of relationships to be borne by people I will never meet.

This knowledge that relationships last; the knowledge that what I do in the here and now with loving and trusting will make a difference in the way my descendants will love and trust ... these are the reasons we forgive. We know that it is our job to do everything we can to strengthen the cable and repair it so that if people were able to look at our relational descendants three generations from now, they would recognize the legacy of love and trust that we gave to them. Forgiveness is about relational survival and health, in the here and now and in the future. It is part of our effort to be remembered in the only way we can be remembered: through relational love and trust.

But it is work that is never quite complete. The effort to restore and salvage trust and love in relationships continues throughout our lifetime and through many generations. We try to do that work on an individual level, on a family level, on a community and national level, and, it is hoped, on a global level. We move back and forth among the stations of forgiveness many times and utilize the stations in many different ways. However, we do the work of forgiveness because in the end, we want to survive. You and I are living testimony to the fact that someone showed enough love, trust, and forgiveness for us to survive. I want to contribute and to make that love and trust better and stronger so that others will survive and prosper.

Also by Terry Hargrave

The Essential Humility of Marriage
Honoring the Third Identity in Couple Therapy

"A wise, balanced, and original approach to fostering a strong "us" in marriage without losing the "you" and "me." Hargrave is onto something nobody in our field has captured before."
— William J. O'Doherty, Ph.D.

This fresh perspective on what makes marriages work will jump-start the efforts of every couples therapist. At its core is Hargrave's message that much of what is currently done in couples therapy misses the point, focusing all attention on the need to accumulate more and more skills and to work toward ever-greater self-actualization. While there is a time and place for both of these concerns, Hargrave suggests that the real answer resides in some new math. Where once we believed that two become one, and then, more recently, that two remained two, Hargrave proposes that in strong marriages, two become three.

The Essential Humility of Marriage explores the landscape of "you," "me," and "we." The book clearly carves out this third identity, and then describes how its expectations and desires can take precedence over those of the individual partners — without taking away from either one. Why the concept of "us" plays such a central role in satisfying marriages is explained, and ways in which therapists can help couples enhance the "us" of their marriage.

ISBN: 1-891944-36-3 • 2000 • Hardcover, 240 pages • $36.95